AMERICAN AND JAPANESE BUSINESS DISCOURSE: A COMPARISON OF INTERACTIONAL STYLES

Haru Yamada

Dept. of East Asian Studies
The University of Arizona

VOLUME XLV in the series
ADVANCES IN DISCOURSE PROCESSES
Roy O. Freedle, Editor

ABLEX PUBLISHING CORPORATION
Norwood, New Jersey

Printed in the United States of America

Library of Congress Cataloging-in-Publication Data

Yamada, Haru.
American and Japanese business discourse : a comparison of interactional styles / Haru Yamada.
p. cm. — (Advances in discouse processes)
Includes bibliographical references and index.
ISBN 0-89391-800-8
1. Business communication—Cross-cultural studies. 2. Oral communication—Cross-cultural studies. 3. Business communication--United States. 4. Business communication—Japan. I. Title.
HF5718.Y36 1992
302.3'5'0952—dc20 91-31749
CIP

Ablex Publishing Corporation
355 Chestnut St.
Norwood, NJ 07648

TO MY FAMILY
AND
FRIENDS IN WASHINGTON, DC

CONTENTS

Preface to the Series

Roy O. Freedle

Series Editor

This series of volumes provides a forum for the cross-fertilization of ideas from a diverse number of disciplines, all of which share a common interest in discourse—be it prose comprehension and recall, dialogue analysis, text grammar construction, computer simulation of natural language, cross-cultural comparisons of communicative competence or other related topics. The problems posed by multisentence contexts and the methods required to investigate them, while not always unique to discourse, are still sufficiently distinct as to benefit from the organized model of scientific interaction made possible by this series.

Scholars working in the discourse area from the perspective of sociolinguistics, psycholinguistics, enthnomethodology and the sociology of language, educational psychology (e.g., teacher-student interaction), the philosophy of language, computational linguistics, and related subareas are invited to submit manuscripts of monograph or book length to the series editor. Edited collections of original papers resulting from conferences will also be considered.

Volumes in the Series

Vol. I. Discourse Production and Comprehension. Roy O. Freedle (Ed.), 1977.

Vol. II.	New Directions in Discourse Processing. Roy O. Freedle (Ed.), 1979.
Vol. III.	The Pear Stories, Cognitive, Cultural, and Linguistic Aspects of Narrative Production. Wallace L. Chafe (Ed.), 1980.
Vol. IV.	Text, Discourse, and Process: Toward a Multidisciplinary Science of Texts. Robert de Beaugrande, 1980.
Vol. V.	Ethnography and Language in Educational Settings. Judith Green & Cynthia Wallat (Eds.), 1981.
Vol. VI.	Latino Language and Communicative Behavior. Richard P. Duran (Ed.), 1981.
Vol. VII.	Narrative Literacy and Face in Interethnic Communication. Ron Scollon & Suzanne Scollon, 1981.
Vol. VIII.	Linguistics and the Professions. Robert J. DiPietro (Ed.), 1982.
Vol. IX.	Spoken and Written Language: Exploring Orality and Literacy. Deborah Tannen (Ed.), 1982.
Vol. X.	Developmental Issues in Discourse. Jonathan Fine & Roy O. Freedle (Eds.), 1983.
Vol. XI.	Text Production: Toward a Science of Composition. Robert de Beaugrande, 1984.
Vol. XII.	Coherence in Spoken and Written Discourse. Deborah Tannen (Ed.), 1984.
Vol. XIII.	The Development of Oral and Written Language in Social Contexts. Anthony D. Pellegrini & Thomas D. Yawkey (Eds.), 1984.
Vol. XIV.	What People Say They Do With Words. Jef Verschueren, 1985.
Vol. XV.	Systemic Perspectives on Discourse, Volume I: Selected Theoretical Papers from the 9th International Systemic Workshop. James D. Benson & William S. Greaves (Eds.), 1985.
Vol. XVI.	Systemic Perspectives on Discourse, Volume 2: Selected Applied Papers from the 9th International Systemic Workshop. James D. Benson & William S. Greaves (Eds.), 1985.
Vol. XVII.	Structures and Procedures of Implicit Knowledge. Arthur C. Graesser & Leslie F. Clark, 1985.
Vol. XVIII.	Contexts of Reading. Carolyn N. Hedley & Anthony N. Baratta (Eds.), 1985.
Vol. XIX.	Discourse and Institutional Authority: Medicine, Education, and Law. Sue Fisher & Alexandra Dundas Todd (Eds.), 1986.
Vol. XX.	Evidentiality: The Linguistic Coding of Epistemology. Wallace Chafe & Johanna Nichols (Eds.), 1986.
Vol. XXI.	The Acquisition of Literacy: Ethnographic Perspectives. Bambi B. Schieffelin & Perry Gilmore (Eds.), 1986.
Vol. XXII.	Cognitive and Linguistic Analyses of Test Performance. Roy O. Freedle & Richard P. Duran (Eds.), 1987.
Vol. XXIII.	Linguistic Action: Some Empirical-Conceptual Studies. Jef Verschueren (Eds.), 1987.
Vol. XXIV.	Text and Epistemology. William Frawley, 1987.
Vol. XXV.	Second Language Discourse: A Textbook of Current Research. Jonathan Fine (Eds.), 1988.

Vol. XXVI. Systemic Functional Approaches to Discourse. James D. Benson & William S. Greaves (Eds.), 1988.
Vol. XXVII. Language Development: Learning Language, Learning Culture. Ruqaiya Hasan & James Martin (Eds.), 1989.
Vol. XXVIII. Multiple Perspective Analyses of Classroom Discourse. Judith L. Green & Judith O. Harker (Eds.), 1988.
Vol. XXIX. Linguistics in Context: Connecting Observation and Understanding. Deborah Tannen (Ed.), 1988.
Vol. XXX. Gender and Discourse: The Power of Talk. Alexandra D. Todd & Sue Fisher (Eds.), 1988.
Vol. XXXI. Cross-Cultural Pragmatics: Requests and Apologies. Shoshana Blum-Kulka, Juliane House & Gabriele Kasper (Eds.), 1989.
Vol. XXXII. Collegial Discourse. Allen D. Grimshaw, 1989.
Vol. XXXIII. Task, Talk, and Text in the Operating Room: A Study in Medical Discourse. Catherine Johnson Pettinari, 1988.
Vol. XXXIV. The Presence of Thought. Introspective Accounts of Reading and Writing. Marilyn S. Sternglass, 1988.
Vol. XXXV. Japanese Conversation: Self-contextualization through Structure and Interactional Management. Senko Kumiya Maynard, 1989.
Vol. XXXVI. Cognitive Assessment of Language and Math Outcomes. Sue Legg & James Algina (Eds.), 1990.
Vol. XXXVII. Pragmatics, Discourse and Text: Some Systemically-inspired Approaches. Erich H. Steiner and Robert Veltman (Eds.), 1988.
Vol. XXXVIII. Conversational Organization and its Development. Bruce Dorval (Ed.), 1990.
Vol. XXIX. Developing Discourse Practices in Adolescence and Adulthood. Richard Beach & Susan Hynds (Eds.), 1990.
Vol. XL. Text and Texture: Patterns of Cohesion. Sally Stoddard, 1991.
Vol XLI. Conversation Analysis of a Marital Therapy Session: The Pursuit of a Therapeutic Agenda. Jerry Edward Gale, 1991.
Vol. XLII. Medical Discourse and Systemic Frames of Comprehension. Ronald J. Chenail, 1991.
Vol. XLIII. What's Going On Here? Complimentary Studies of Professional Talk. Allen Day Grimshaw et al., 1992.
Vol. XLIV. Ambiguous Harmony, Family Talk in America. Hervé Varenne, 1992.
Vol. XLV. American and Japanese Business Discourse: A Comparison of Interactional Styles. Haru Yamada, 1992.
Vol. XLVI. Scientific Discourse: An Analysis of Biomedical Journal Articles' Discussion Sections. Betty Lou DuBois, 1992.
Vol. XLVII. Repetition in Discourse: Interdisciplinary Perspectives, Volume 1. Barbara Johnstone (Ed.), 1992.
Vol. XLVIII. Repetition in Discourse: Interdisciplinary Perspectives, Volume 2. Barbara Johnstone (Ed.), 1992.
Vol. XLIX. Word Choice and Narration in Academic Lectures: An Essay on Artistic Language Use. Barbara Strodt-López, 1992.

ACKNOWLEDGMENTS

I am greatly indebted to a number of very generous people who helped me at various stages of this research. I begin by expressing lasting gratitude to Deborah Tannen, my mentor and teacher. Her influence on my work goes back to a cross-cultural communication class at Georgetown University in 1982. At that time, she planted in me the seeds of what turned out to be an irreversible interest in sociolinguistics and cross-cultural analysis. During my graduate studies, she again taught, advised, and guided me through the process of analysis and writing. My development as a sociolinguist is due in great part to her insight and inspiration. From beginning to end, Deborah Tannen has been an unending source of motivation and direction.

I also thank James Alatis and Miwa Nishimura for their useful input in the earlier phases; Neal Norrick, Senko Maynard, Rebecca Oxford, and Robert Di Pietro for their comments on drafts of the book in the latter phases. I thank, in particular, Neal Norrick, who gave invaluable, detailed suggestions and pointers on two complete drafts. I also appreciate the insight of Senko Maynard, whose pioneering work in Japanese conversation stimulates, challenges, and directs my own ongoing analysis of Japanese conversation. These scholars and others continue to inform my work; however, I am solely responsible for any shortcomings or inadequacies remaining.

My sincere thanks also go to all eight participants of the business meetings for allowing a linguist to poke around during their hectic business schedules.

I also thank my parents. Raising me with one foot in the United States and the other in Japan, they taught me the most important goal of comparative sociolinguistic analysis: Respect and understand people of different cultures. As difficult as it is to abide by this principle, I have tried to do so here. My parents' unconditional support in this endeavor have strengthened my resolve to do so. I thank them for their priceless and gentle guidance through the path to finding the splendor of different ways.

Finally, I thank all of my friends for their emotional support. I especially thank my best friends, Kyoko Takashi and Bruno Mathieu, for lending me their shoulders and sharing my laughter. Their friendship gave me much of the courage and tenacity that I needed for the completion of this book.

PERMISSION

Two papers that contain analyses similar to those in this book have been published. These are: "Topic and turn distribution in business meetings: American versus Japanese strategies" (TEXT 10.3.271-95, 1990); "Topic shifts in American and Japanese business conversations" (Georgetown Journal of Languages and Linguistics 1.2.249-56, 1990). In addition, "Point-making in American and Japanese business meetings" will appear in the proceedings of the Seventeenth LACUS Forum in 1991. I thank the publishers and editors for their permission to use similar material in this book.

PREFACE

As the frequency of political and economic dialogue between the United States and Japan increases, so do the opportunites for contact and interaction between the peoples of these two nations. Increased contact, however, has not necessarily led to cross-cultural understanding between the United States and Japan. To the extent that the present relationship has evolved from one of enemies in a world war to a relatively peaceful trade relationship, the partnership has improved considerably. Even so, minor misunderstandings still continue to occur, accumulate, and escalate to uncomfortable levels of stereotyping: "Japanese are patronizing, evasive, and inscrutable"; "Americans are aggressive, lazy, and selfish."

In many ways, the stereotypes of today are simply old ones disguised in new forms. In fact, both Americans and Japanese invoke war metaphors to characterize the present trade conflict between the United States and Japan. For example, in a county meeting that addressed resident resentment of a plan to open a Japanese school in a Maryland county, a resident was noted as saying: "They [the Japanese] are taking over. We won the war militarily, let's not lose it economically" (Leff, *Washington Post*, 9/3/89). The image of the Japanese as an "economic monster" is further reflected in public opinion polls in the United States that indicate that "Americans now view Tokyo's economic power as a greater threat to the United States than the Soviet military'' (*Newsweek*, 4/2/90:19). Similarly, also likening the present trade conflict between the two nations to a war, the self-confident younger generation in Japan is smugly satisfied with the feeling that it has emerged victoriously in the so-called trade war or '*nichibei sensoo*' ('the war between the Japan and the United States'). Previously viewed as a ''big brother'' nation, the Japanese now allegedly regard America as a land of lazy crybabies (*Newsweek*, 4/2/90). Because history has shown that cross-cultural stereotypes result not only in devastating and irrevocable consequences, but also in a prolonged and profound mutual blindness, cross-cultural understanding between the United States and Japan—as well as among other nations—is of critical importance.

In the tradition of interactional sociolinguistics begun by Gumperz (1982a) and extended by Tannen (1984a), researchers have shown that cross-cultural stereotypes occur in part because different groups evaluate each other on the basis of different cultural assumptions and expectations about how to interact and communicate. Moreover, interactional sociolinguists have also shown that interactants manage a variety of conversational strategies to reflect their cultural expectations for interaction. As a general goal of this book, then, I compare American and Japanese conversational strategies in intracultural business meetings to explore differences in their respective expectations for interaction, and plausible sources for cross-cultural stereotyping. More specifically, I focus upon the different strategies that American and Japanese bank officers use to manage conversational topics. In the following section, I sketch the organizational framework of the book, outline the major contents of each chapter, and conclude with a preliminary introduction to the data and a key to transcription conventions.

ORGANIZATION, CONTENTS, AND DATA

The book is divided into three parts. The first part (Chapters 1 and 2) provide a theoretical and ethnographic background to the analytic chapters (Chapters 3 through 5). Following this second part is a final chapter which discusses areas for future research.

In Chapter 1, I discuss the key concepts of interactional sociolinguistics (Gumperz, 1982a; Tannen 1984a) in which my study is based: context, interpretive frames, and sharedness. I then describe the model Cross-Talk (Gumperz, Jupp and Roberts, 1979) used as a guide for comparing the American and Japanese meetings. I conclude this chapter with a discussion about the forces that helped motivate the study.

In Chapter 2, I provide an ethnographic background for the subsequent analytic chapters by comparing American and Japanese expectations for interaction, and I describe the data in further detail. In discussing American and Japanese interactional expectations, I first examine the cultural context and then consider two continua of interactional expectations: the Individual-Group Dimension, and the Talk-Silence Dimension. A number of studies comparing American and Japanese behavior suggest that while Americans emphasize the interactional mode of individuality, the Japanese stress the mode of collectivity (for example, see Fallows, 1989; Kume, 1985; Moeran, 1986; Nakane, 1986; Wagatsuma, 1985). Likewise, research comparing Americans and Japanese along the Talk-Silence continuum (for example, Doi, 1982; Mizutani, 1979) finds Americans to favor, but Japanese to distrust, talk. Consulting the literature, I probe further into the nature of these preferred cultural modes of interaction.

I then discuss how the Individual-Group and Talk-Silence dimensions coalesce to create interactive expectations for each group. I define the integrated expectations for interaction in terms of different paradoxes presented to the Americans and Japanese respectively. That is, although Americans give prominence to the individual in interaction, they still need to relate to and understand other group members. This interactional tension guides American interactants to use conversational strategies that respond to an expectation which I call "within-group independence." On the other hand, the Japanese have a different dilemma: while talk is viewed as an unreliable medium for communication, interactions often require talk. To respond to this double bind, Japanese interactants use conversational strategies which minimize the emphasis on talk and thereby strengthen the relationship among group members. I call this interactive expectation "nonconfrontation." Here my use of the term "nonconfrontation" does not imply that Japanese interactions are void of conflict. In fact, in my analysis, I illustrate many of the disagreements that emerge in the Japanese meeting. Rather, my notion of "nonconfrontation" is a method of managing conflict and other interactional phenomena which arise in Japanese conversations.

Comparative studies of American and Japanese business also report that there are differences in what Americans and Japanese expect from a business encounter (for example, see Graham, cited in Pfeiffer, 1988; Kume, 1985; McCreary, 1986; Ouchi, 1981). These differences find their roots in a general difference about how to conduct business—a difference in how to reach decisions, and a difference in how to build business relationships. That is, by resolving individual differences in opinions and suggestions, American business people often expect to reach decisions in a meeting. Japanese business people, on the other hand, make their decisions outside the meeting through concensus. Furthermore, Americans often separate business and personal relations, but Japanese do not. Such differences about what Americans and Japanese expect from a meeting account in part for the different ways in which the meetings are structured. Thus, in Chapter 2, I also allude to the comparative literature on American and Japanese business practices.

I present the comparisons of topic-management strategies in Chapters 3 through 5. These strategies are not by any means exhaustive; they merely show one way in which Americans and Japanese manage their topics differently. For all comparisons, however, I find that the American and Japanese bank officers use different strategies to manage their topics. Moreover, each strategy reflects the underlying expectations for interaction that I discuss in Chapter 2: Americans expect "within-group independence," the expression of individuality within the confines of the group, but Japanese expect "nonconfrontation," the use of talk to maximize the collective integration of the group.

Chapter 3 compares how the American and Japanese participants open and shift topics; Chapter 4, the way they distribute topical talk, and make points about a topic; Chapter 5, the way listeners express support. In general, in the American meeting, I find that a single participant opens, delivers, and closes his or her own topic. By contrast, in the Japanese meeting, I find that any participant can raise and contribute to a topic, and that topics are not verbally concluded, but separated by silences. In addition, the American officers organize their topics and points in a linear, temporal order, but the Japanese organize theirs circularly. Finally, I show that the Japanese express their listenership through "back-channel cues" (Yngve, 1970) (short vocalizations, such as "uhuh" or "mhm" in English and "*nm, nm, nm*" in Japanese) much more often than the Americans, and that the two groups use such back-channels in different topical contexts. Following the analyses, I conclude the book with a short discussion about the possible areas for future research in cross-cultural communication and conversational strategies.

The primary data are tape-recorded intracultural American and Japanese bank officers' meetings. These meetings took place in two international financial institutions in San Francisco in the summer of 1988. In the American meeting, the language of interaction is American English; in the Japanese meeting, it is Japanese. Both the 27-minute American meeting and the 20-minute Japanese meeting have three participants, and are examples of weekly meetings. I asked a participant in each meeting to tape-record the meeting as a personal favor. After they secured the consent of the other participants, they then tape-recorded the meetings as they naturally occurred. My only other requests to the participant responsible for recording were: ethnographic profiles of the meeting members, and follow-up conversations in the future. Each participant responsible for recording collected the requested ethnographic profiles, and reported in our first follow-up conversation that the meetings were "typical" weekly meetings.

Interspersed throughout Chapters 3 and 4, and more extensively in Chapter 5, I use examples from backup data collected in two American-Japanese cross-cultural meetings conducted in English. Both meetings were again recorded by a participant as a personal favor: One cross-cultural meeting (hereafter referred to as the "Corporate Banking" meeting) was recorded by the same participant who recorded the Japanese meeting, the other (hereafter referred to as the "Personnel" meeting) was recorded by another Japanese bank officer. The cross-cultural meetings were also recorded in the summer of 1988, in the same financial institution where the Japanese meeting was recorded. The 28-minute Personnel meeting with two participants, and the 46-minute Corporate Banking meeting with four participants are also examples of weekly meetings, and were recorded in the same way as the intracultural meetings. I discuss the participants in the intracultural and cross-cultural meetings in further detail in the Chapter 2.

In sum, my primary goal is to demonstrate that the American

and Japanese bank officers in my study use different topic-management strategies, and that such differences arise in part because Americans and Japanese respond to different interactional expectations. Moreover, I suggest that different topic-management strategies, though coherent intraculturally, create problems in cross-cultural communication. As Americans and Japanese each use native strategies to communicate across groups, they both use their own methods of interpretation and thus frequently misunderstand one another. The result is often a confirmation of previously held misconceptions and stereotypes. Today, most of us interact with members of different sociolinguistic groups. As global interdependency increases, it behooves us to join forces in cross-cultural understanding, empathy, and respect. I hope that this modest study will contribute to this common human goal.

KEY TO TRANSCRIPTION CONVENTIONS

>	falling tone contour
<	rising tone contour
:	lengthened sounds
'	ommitted sounds
[	latched/overlapping speech
–	clipped speech
,	discernible pause, between 0.5 sec. and 1.0 sec. in duration
.	discernible pause, between 1.0 sec. and 1.5 sec. in duration
{ }	discernible pause, greater than 1.5 seconds, actually indicated with figure
[ ]	nonlinguistic sounds, comment on quality of talk
CAPS	emphatic stress
!	exclamation
bold	point of analysis

TRANSCRIPTION CONVENTIONS FOR JAPANESE

1. I use the Hepburn style of romanization in the Japanese transcription.
2. I provide a word-by-word gloss directly below the transcribed Japanese. I then translate the excerpt in entirety below. For the most part, the translations are idiomatic; however, I translate some parts literally to preserve the Japanese meaning.
3. Markers:

D	direct object
E	emphatic
I	indirect object
L	locative
NEG	negative
P	possessive
PH	phrase-final
PU	purpose
Q	question
QU	quotative
S	subject
T	topic
TFD	time-frame (de)
TFN	time-frame (ni)
TO	toward
U	use (by means of)

CHAPTER 1

INTERACTIONAL UNDERSTANDING FROM THE NATIVE'S POINT OF VIEW

The past half-century has given rise to a debate among linguists regarding the role of context in shaping meaningful language. In contrast to behaviorists who argue that language results from constant environmental reinforcement, rationalists contend that language is generated from within the rational, human mind, through logic-governed linguistic rules. In structuring meaning in language, behaviorists regard the environment as primary; rationalists, as auxiliary.

As the debate continues, a new group, which Shweder (1984) calls the "romantic rebellion," has joined the discussion. The proponents of the romantic rebellion oppose the view taken by rationalists; they argue for the significant influence of the local and cultural context on language. This perspective provides the most general direction for this book. Language is not merely "out there" in the environment, waiting to make its mark on someone, nor does it simply reside in someone's head. As Becker (1988), Geertz (1973), and Hymes (1986) among others have aptly described, language is a symbolic expression of cultural experience made real in an actual and particular context of interactional use. Language is the expression and experience of people; it simultaneously glues people together, and yet sets them apart from one another.

The debate has produced a wealth of scholars in a number of

different fields, offering several traditions for the study of meaning and culture in face-to-face interaction, or conversation. Scholars from each tradition have contributed to our present understanding of conversation. Philosophers and pragmaticists (Brown and Levinson, 1987; Grice, 1975; Leech 1983; Schiffrin, 1985; Sperber and Wilson, 1986) have shown that participants use conversation as a cooperative venture to communicate meaning beyond propositional and literal meanings. Sociologists and ethnomethodologists (Garfinkel, 1967; Heritage, 1984; Sacks, Schegloff, and Jefferson, 1974) have demonstrated that conversational structures are systematically organized in socially meaningful ways. Anthropologists and ethnographers (Gumperz, 1972, 1982a, 1982c; Gumperz and Cook-Gumperz, 1982a; Gumperz and Hymes, 1986; Gumperz, Jupp, and Roberts, 1979; Hymes, 1964; 1986; Saville-Troike, 1982) have illustrated that conversation varies according to ethnographic variants, and that the same sociocultural experience is categorized through linguistic variables in different ways. Placing linguistic analyses within social and ethnographic contexts, interactional sociolinguists (Gumperz, 1977, 1982a; Tannen 1984a, 1989, 1990) have demonstrated that conversation is imbued with sociocultural symbolism, such that the subtle hues of conversational meaning cannot be derived by examining linguistic features in isolation. The research of scholars has thus given rise to a view that conversation is cooperative, communicative of sociocultural meanings, and variable across different sociocultural groups.

INTERACTIONAL SOCIOLINGUISTICS

The conversation analysis in this book is grounded in the theoretical framework of interactional sociolinguistics. Developed by Gumperz (1977, 1982a) and extended by Tannen (1984a), the tradition investigates areas of inquiry beyond conversation, contributing to the development of theories and methods in discourse, comparative ethnography, and cross-cultural communication. An overarching premise of interactional sociolinguistics is that meaning is interactional; it is based on shared expectations and is interpretable only in the context of interaction.

In the following section, I discuss this premise, describing what I consider to be the critical ingredients of theory and method in interactional sociolinguistics: context, interpretive frames, and (un)sharedness of interactional assumptions and expectations. I then present the model, Cross-talk (Gumperz, Jupp, and Roberts, 1979), which I use as a guide in comparing the American and Japanese business meetings in this book. Finally, I outline the motivating forces for the study.

Context

Context is at the core of social interaction and is therefore primary to the investigation of language in face-to-face interaction. The centrality of meaning-in-context in conversation is what Garfinkel (1986) and Sacks (1986) refer to as "situated meaning," and has been discussed extensively by a number of researchers including but not limited to Blom and Gumperz (1986), Geertz (1984), Goffman (1972), Gumperz (1982a), Hall (1977), Sacks (1986), Schiffrin (1987), Tannen (1984a) (for a survey on "context" and "contextual features," see Brown and Yule, 1983). As put succinctly by Bateson (1979:15): "Without context, words and actions have no meaning at all."

But what exactly is meaning-in-context? I argue that meaning-in-context is a synthesis of several interactive relationships, which in a complex web of association with interactants, collaboratively compose interactional meaning. In order to explain this relationship, I allocate "meaning-in-context" to three concentric spheres, with the cultural context at the core, followed by the context of encounter, and the context of conversation, respectively.

I view this relationship of meaning-in-context as analogous to a system of sound waves traveling through the air; in a simultaneous instant, the contextual spheres are mutually influential. The influence of each context is therefore implicationally bidirectional. In other words, the cultural context influences the contexts of encounter and conversation, as the context of encounter influences the conversational context. However, a reverse implicational process proceeds concurrently; the context of the encounter also influences the cultural context, as the conversational context influences the contexts of encounter and culture. Thus, contextual influence is interactive as shown in Figure 1.1.

If Figure 1.1 is seen as the context necessary for a single

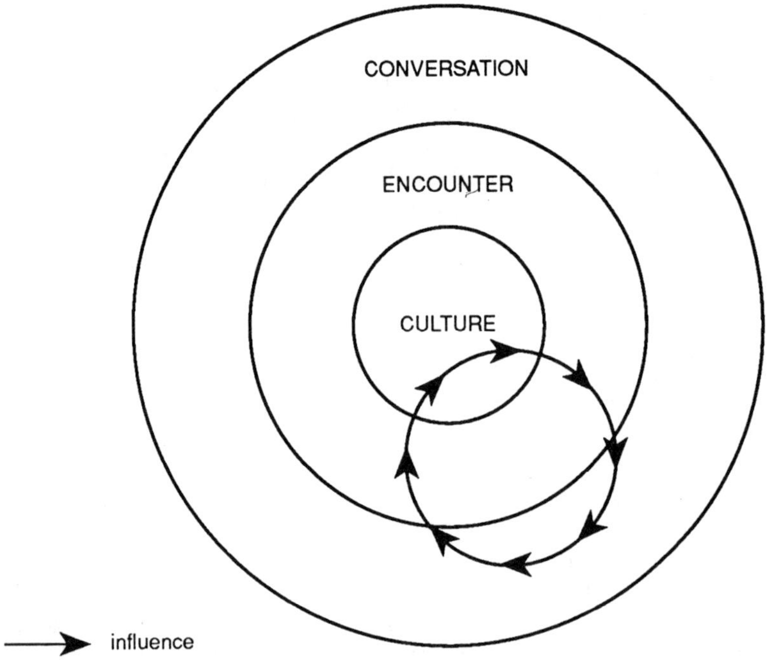

FIGURE 1.1. INTERACTIONAL CONTEXT.

person, the complexity of interrelationships in interaction mushrooms as each person's bundled contextual sphere overlaps with and interacts with others'. In a somewhat similar description, S. Maynard (1989:4-5) characterizes the formal mechanisms of "self-contextualization": "the on-going process of continually defining oneself in relation to one's interactional environment." According to S. Maynard (1989:4), the processes of self-contextualization involves two interacting stages which she calls "contextual interpretation", "the participant's understanding of actual signs and other abstract structural and interactional knowledge labeled as elements of conversation" and "contextual transformation," the transformation of ideas to suit a situation of talk or context.

My representation of meaning-in-context is also broadly similar to Hymes' (1986) classification of social units: the speech situation, the speech event, and the speech act. However, Hymes' goal is to differentiate various levels of social units for analysis, whereas my goal in this section is to describe the varying degrees of meaning-in-context. Thus, although I have segregated the spheres of context for the purpose of explanation, in interaction, the spheres are mutually influential; they are necessarily overlapping and interdependent.

In the following, I give broad descriptions of each of the spheres. Before beginning, however, I emphasize two important points. First, while I separate each of the spheres for the purpose of discussion, an opportunity for the accomplishment of interactional meaning in actual interactions becomes possible only when all spheres are resident concurrently. Second, I distinguish each sphere not in terms of a difference in quantity (as in a measurable unit), but rather in terms of a difference in qualitative relationships. For example, if we think of each sphere as a friend, each of the friends can be distinguished from one another in terms of a difference in friend relations: Friend A and Friend B have a different relationship from Friend B and Friend C, and from Friend A and Friend C. Thus, the spheres are distinguishable because they differ in the way they relate to one another. Although there is extensive literature that describes "discourse" and other sociolinguistic and social constructs in terms of units (for example, see Brown and Yule, 1983; Gumperz, 1982a; Hymes, 1986; and S. Maynard, 1989), Bateson (1979) reminds us that we often see distinctions through difference in relationship; a difference of quality, rather than amount.

The following order of presentation is arbitrary, and I begin with the middle sphere, the context of encounter. The term "encounter" has been variously labeled and defined (for example, Blom & Gumperz, 1986; Geertz, 1984; Gumperz, 1982a; Hall, 1977; Sacks, 1986). I borrow Goffman's (1972:63) definition of an encounter: "an environment of mutual monitoring possibilities, anywhere within which an individual will find himself accessible to the naked senses of all others who are present, and similarly find them accessible to him." My only modification is the substitution of "interactant" for "individual" because I use the word "individual" later on in a different sense. Goffman's context-based description of encounter assumes the presence of other contextual spheres. Thus, in this view as well as in mine, the encounter is seen as the context of the immediate environment in which interactants organize themselves. It is the context in which interactants experience and make use of their know-how of a particular sociocultural milieu, and participate in the interaction through meaningful "presentations of the self" (Goffman, 1959).

Interactants express such "presentations of the self" through language (Goffman, 1959). As one among four of the critical "assumptions of discourse analysis" (Schiffrin, 1987:3-6), Schiffrin argues that language is always communicative. The communicative context of language in face-to-face interaction is, then, what I refer to as the context of conversation. In the context of conversation, interactants associate informative pieces of "conversational data," which include nonverbal and nonsyntactic information, as well as verbally- and syntactically-encoded data. Although nonverbal and nonsyntactic data, such as silence, have typically been considered as "extralinguistic" in traditional linguistics, and hence, not directly relevant to the study of language, Bateson (1979), S. Maynard (1989), Philips (1985), and Tannen (1985c), among others inform us that such surface data also have meaning-in-context.

Associated pieces of conversational data are therefore meaningful only in the context of the conversation, which in turn relies on the context of a particular sociocultural encounter. Thus, the encounter guides the conversation, but conversely, the conversation also defines the encounter, as interactants use the context of conversation to make sense of the encounter. In short, the context of conversation is necessary for a meaningful encounter, and vice versa.

At the core of interactional context is culture. The cultural context is the broadest yet most central, the most hidden and yet most relevent. Its nuclear position makes the cultural context pivotal; the "heart" of an interaction. Anthropologists and sociologists (and recently, sociolinguists) have grappled with the conceptualization of the term "culture" for some time (for example, see Geertz, 1973; Shweder & LeVine, 1984). For this study, I borrow Geertz's (1973:89) description: "an historically transmitted pattern of meanings embodied in symbols, a system of inherited conceptions expressed in symbolic forms by means of which men communicate, perpetuate, and develop their knowledge about and attitudes towards life." Thus, culture is both historic and immediate; it defines a conversational encounter, but is also redefined with each new encounter and conversation.

In sum, each context is necessary for interaction, and interactional meaning is plausible only when all meaning-in-context spheres are resident. In interaction, then, participants make use of the dynamic contexts of conversation, encounter, and culture, and also rely on their experience of past contexts. Doing so not only helps define the ongoing encounter, but allows participants to interpret the interaction. This is the subject of the following section on interpretive frames.

Interpretive Frames

While I have made the point that context is a basic part of interactional meaning, the question still remains: How do interactants actually "understand" such meaning? The answer is found in part, in a method of "understanding" defined by interactional sociolinguists called "interpretive frames."

The term "frame" has been used variously in sociology, sociolinguistics, anthropology, cognitive science, and psychology, and its definition varies accordingly (for a review, see Tannen, 1979, 1985b). Recently, perspectives of the notion of the "frame" have diverged into two distinctive branches, with cognitive scientists and psychologists on the one hand, and sociologists, sociolinguists, and anthroplogists on the other. In cognitive science and psychology, Schank and Abelson (1977) designed a model known as "script theory," which describes how people activate formal properties of knowledge structures (a stereotyped sequence of events and actions) stored in the mind. Such stereotyped knowledge structures have since been referred to as "frame," "script," and "schema" (Tannen, 1985b). In sociology, Goffman (1974), building on Batesons' (1972) anthropological notion of the "frame," formulated a method of analysis for frames as they are used in interaction. In the sociological perspective, a "frame" is an interactive set of principles which govern a particular situation.

Interactional sociolinguists further built upon the sociological conceptualization of "frame" (Gumperz, 1982a; Tannen, 1979, 1985b; Tannen and Wallat, 1987). Also called "schemata" (Gumperz, 1982a), and "superordinate message" (Goffman, 1974), a "frame" refers to an interpreted mode of interactional understanding: "a set of expectations which rests on previous experience" (Gumperz, 1982a:102). A frame describes how participants understand and evaluate "what is going on" (Gumperz, 1982a) in an interaction, and is always "interactive" (Tannen, 1985b), as well as "interpretive" (Gumperz, 1982a). In the following section, I discuss these key aspects of the frame.

First, while a frame occurs in a particular context, contexts change with each instant. Thus, a participant's frame at a particular point in the interaction is a frozen image of cumulative interpreting experiences up until that point. However, because the interaction is dynamic, frames are interactive and ever-changing. They are constantly redefined from moment to moment in a single interaction, as well as from combined redefinitions over a period of time. In short, a frame is a set of expectations based on the cumulative experience of culture- and encounter-specific conversations.

Moreover, interactants intend for frames to be interpreted, and actually interpret frames by relying on accumulated experiences and producing alternative ways to make sense of the interaction. The "interepretive frame" is, then, a method of interpretation; a systematic "matching" of expectations with moment-by-moment conversation. Interactants therefore use interpretive frames to categorize and evaluate the conversation, as well as what the conversation might reflect about participants in the interaction. In sum, interactants use interpretive frames to bond with the conversation and other participants, so that they may mutually interpret and negotiate interactional meaning.

Sharedness

With Gumperz's notion of an interpretive frame, I argued that interactants rely on expectations based on their past experiences to make sense of the present. From this principle, Gumperz (1982a) further asserts that similar past experiences motivate similar interpretive frames. Because no two people have identical experiences, each person has a slightly different frame for interpreting the same interactional phenomena. However, because our past experience includes a conventionalized, cultural know-how (embedded in the cultural context discussed earlier), members of a cultural group share interpretive frames.

Gumperz (1982a) takes this argument one step further, describing how participants signal interpretive frames. Referred to as "contextualization cues," "any feature of linguistic form that contributes to the signalling of contextual presuppositions" (Gumperz, 1982a:131), these cues signal the intended interpretive frame, and allow coparticipants to evaluate the signaler's intentions, and respond on the basis of that evaluation. However, the interpretation of contextualization cues which Gumperz (1982a) calls "conversational inference" is dependent on the extent to which participants share culture-

and encounter-specific interpretive frames, or what Gumperz (1982a) refers to as "contextualization conventions." Thus, interpretation is facilitated when contextualization conventions are shared; the interaction then makes sense to the participants; it "feels right."

The flip side of cultural sharedness is unsharedness. Cultural unsharedness creates dissimilar interpretive frames among interactants which, in turn, motivate a different set of contextualization conventions. With this theoretical background, Gumperz, Jupp, and Roberts (1979) designed their model for cross-cultural comparison. I discuss the model, used as a guide for this study, following an example where I apply the previously mentioned theoretical concepts.

Clues of Interactional Understanding: An Example

Thus far, I have extracted several aspects of "interaction" to discuss its significance in the analysis of face-to-face interaction. I argued that an abstract concept such as "context" is important for our understanding of an interaction because we do not understand conversational data in a void. I also suggested that the notion of a "frame" is essential in our understanding of how we interpret the ever-changing moments of an interaction, and that there must be a degree of "sharedness" for interactional understanding. In short, I argued that such ingredients must be present in an interaction for it to be "meaningful," and for participants to share meaning in the ongoing interaction, and understand one another.

In the following section, I demonstrate the importance of these concepts with an excerpt taken from the American business meeting analyzed for the present study. Here, two loan officers, Lynn and Karen, are finishing a discussion about Company G's buyout of another company. As a final item to be discussed, this deal was "on hold" for some time, but is now closed; it is "off inventory." Example 1.1 shows the final exchange which concludes the discussion on Company G. To preserve anonymity in this example, and those hereafter, I use pseudonyms for all companies and names of individuals discussed over the course of the meetings.

Example 1.1

1	Lynn	yeah< uhh so that- that's- it, it's CLOSed on our
2		books for right now< and until, yeah< we c-
3		ever hear again<
4	Karen	m<kay>
		[
5	Lynn	uhm< , fro- from Chicago>
6	Karen	so it's off inventory>
7	Lynn	so it's off inventory> , completely>
8	Karen	I wish my mind would go off inventory>, ok>
9	Lynn	ok< [laughs] so< , yup<

The excerpt in Example 1.1 illustrates how Karen and Lynn, as well as you, as a reader, and I, as a writer have employed the concepts of context, interpretive frame, and sharedness to understand this portion of the conversation. First, without all the interactional contexts, conversation, encounter, and culture, any one of the utterances is incomprehensible. Even Lynn's longest string of utterances (lines 1 through 3), "yeah, uhh so that- that's- it, it's CLOSed on our books for right now, and until, yeah, we c- ever hear again" seems nonsensical out of context. I gave part of the interactional when I introduced the excerpt. The conversational context is a discussion about Company G's buyout of another company. As Karen and Lynn talk about "Company G" as a final item in the meeting proceedings, they work toward an understanding that the case of "Company G" is no longer "on-hold"; "it is off inventory." The context of the encounter is the weekly business meeting among American bank officers in which relevant deals are reported and discussed.

In the context of culture, we have culture-specific assumptions about what constitutes a legitimate meeting, and expectations about how an American business meeting should proceed. If our expecations about American business meetings are similar to those of Karen's and Lynn's, we may notice a shift in frames in Example 1.1. That shift occurs as Karen says (line 8), "I wish my mind would go off inventory"; the frame of discussing a specific business venture shifts with Karen's play on words "off inventory" to a more personal, joke-frame. The shift in frames is negotiable within the context of the American business meeting because Lynn is not obliged to accept Karen's comment as a joke. However, because "Company G" is the last item-at-hand which warrants discussion in the meeting, Karen's joke is appropriately placed in the conversational contexts of this American business meeting. That is, as Lynn recognizes Karen's joke with a laugh, she acknowledges the shift in frames which allows the participants to move out of the context of the meeting to resume their daily activities. Thus, Lynn's acceptance of the joke produces a shared and negotiated meaning in the interactional exchange between Karen and Lynn, and at another level, in our interpretation of the excerpt.

Our interpretation of the shift in frames, and our judgment that it is socially appropriate is therefore only possible if our expectations about cultural and business behavior are shared. To "interpret" what is going on in the exchange in Example 1.1, then, we jointly interweave multiple interactional contexts to craft a frame to interpret the excerpt. In turn, the extent to which our interpretations are shared is dependent upon our sharedness of assumptions about cultural and business interaction.

In sum, I illustrated how an analyst might apply concepts such as "context," "interpretive frame," and "sharedness" to uncover some clues of interactional understanding. A note of caution, however, is that while these ingredients are useful for the analyst, and necessary for meaningful interaction, they do not in and of themselves constitute interactional understanding. As analysts we can only sketch a picture, because no formula composed of dissected pieces equals interactional understanding. Moreover, in interaction, participants do not "tally up" contexts. Rather, because interactions are rhythmic, aesthetic, and laden with the subjectivity of human experience, a moment of interactional understanding is more like, to use Geertz' (1984:135) words, "grasping a proverb, catching an illusion, seeing a joke—or, . . . reading a poem."[1]

THE MODEL: CROSS-TALK

My method for comparing American and Japanese participant interaction in intracultural business meetings is guided by the structural model of Cross-Talk (Gumperz, Jupp, & Roberts,

[1] Geertz (1984) uses this analogy to describe the inner lives of natives.

1979). The model is part of Gumperz's larger body of research (Gumperz, 1982a), and was specifically devised to uncover why different groups often evaluate each other negatively. Originally designed as a training manual and video for British restaurant employers and Indian employees, Gumperz, Jupp, and Roberts (1979) examined why Britishers (employers and customers) felt that Indians (waiters and waitresses) were "rude," and, conversely, why Indians felt discriminated against by Britishers. The answers became the pillars of the model: Cross-cultural difficulties arise because different cultural groups have different "ways of speaking" reflecting differences in their respective expectations about appropriate behavior for interaction. Thus, although both the Britishers and the Indians were interacting through the medium of the English language, cultural differences manifested in different "ways of speaking," otherwise called "discourse/conversational strategies" (Gumperz, 1982a), and "conversational style" (Tannen, 1984a). I hereafter use the term "conversational strategies" for "ways of speaking."

Theory and Application

The Cross-Talk model characterizes three interdependent levels for cross-cultural comparison. These levels range from the most hidden cultural assumptions to the more observable ways of speaking:

1. different cultural assumptions about the situation and appropriate behavior and intentions within it
2. different ways of structuring information or an argument in a conversation
3. different ways of speaking: the use of a different set of unconscious linguistic conventions (Gumperz & Cook-Gumperz, 1982a, p. 12).

This model is important as a theoretical framework for cross-cultural comparison, as an exercise in comparative and interpretive method, and for its utility in uncovering the basis for difficulties experienced in cross-cultural interaction. As a theoretical framework, each level of the model reflects the underlying concepts of interactional sociolinguistics described earlier. An interactional context interpreted through shared frames is present at all levels of the model for each intracultural group compared. Thus, the model accounts for how "context," "interpretive frames," and "sharedness" influence interactional behavior.

In addition, the model challenges several widely accepted assumptions about cross-cultural interaction. One commonly held belief is that cross-cultural misunderstandings result from a nonnative speaker's inability to generate nativelike phonological and syntactic constructions. For example, I recently had a phone conversation with a Japanese exbusiness associate. After a few minutes of exchanging pleasantries, I asked him about how things were going in his company (a joint-venture American-Japanese company where I had been employed). His response was, "*aa aikawarazu, rei no komyunikeishon no mondai de zuibun atama o itametemasu yo*" ("well, as always, we're beating our heads in with the usual communication problems"). I knew about the "communication problems" because when I worked at the company, I was unofficially assigned the role of cross-cultural interpreter. Still, out of curiosity, I asked what kinds of problems these were. His response was, "*dakara, datte, eigo ga muzukashii kara sa*" ("because, *BECAUSE* English is so difficult"). Further probing, I asked, "What's so difficult about English?" To which he responded in an annoyed tone, "*futsuu no nihonjin no shita tte yuu no wa ne, Haru-chan no mitai ni mawaranainda yo*" ("normal Japanese peoples' tongues don't roll around like YOURS" [emphatic]).[2] This implied that Americans and Japanese have cross-cultural communication problems because Japanese pronounce things funny!

In conversation, native speakers easily identify "foreigners" through readily observable "accents" and nonnative grammatical constructions. Thus, when communication problems arise in cross-cultural interaction, participants frequently attribute misunderstandings to the nonnative speaker's inability to master native "pronunciation" and "grammar." While nativelike mastery of pronunciation and grammar facilitate cross-

[2] Unlike American English, the Japanese /r/ is typically flapped, producing a sound that is similar to the sound produced instead of [t] or [d] in words like "butter" or "ladder" in American English. Because the "r-sound" of American English does not exist in Japanese, the /r/ in American English sounds extremely prominent to a Japanese layman; American English sounds as if it were full of "r-sounds." When a non-English speaking Japanese mimicks English, the gibberish that s/he produces is often a string of "r-sounds," much like the sound one would make imitating the noise of a motor.

cultural interaction, they do not constitute native proficiency, and cross-cultural miscommunication often results from more hidden differences in culture-specific contextualization conventions.

A multitude of studies done in the tradition of interactional sociolinguistics and ethnography of communication show that cross-cultural problems arise because of differences in expectations about how to interact, how to organize communication, and how to use cues that reflect such underlying values and organization. Scollon and Scollon's (1981) study of northern Athabaskans and monolingual English speakers, and Philips (1983) study of Anglo teachers and Warm Spring Indian students show that each group has different assumptions about how much or how little to speak in a particular situation, and about how social relations define who should speak, and when. Gumperz, Aulakh, and Kaltman (1982), Mishra (1982) and Gumperz and Cook-Gumperz (1982b) show how Indian English speakers and British English speakers have different ways of organizing their communication, and cuing such organizational structures. Similarly, Tannen (1981b, 1984b) shows how New York Jewish speakers of English have different expectations about interaction than Californians of Christian backgrounds: about when and what to say, about how talk should be paced, and about how direct or indirect that talk should be. These are among many studies that show how different groups use different contextualization conventions, and how such differences are a potential source of cross-cultural miscommunication.

Another widely held misconception is that one's own way of making sense of the interaction is the "only" and "correct" way. This assumption is reinforced by members of the same cultural group because the way of making sense of interactions is shared. Because each intracultural group member is convinced that their way is *the* way, when cross-cultural interactants encounter different contextualization conventions, they often evaluate each other negatively. Different expectations about how to interact, how to organize information, and how to signal those organizational structures and expectations result in the negative labels we commonly refer to as stereotypes. The "other people" are labeled as "stupid," "illogical," "inscrutable," "reticent," "pushy," and so forth.

Again, there are many studies in interactional sociolinguistics that show how differences at each level of the Cross-Talk model lead to such cross-cultural stereotyping. For example,

Tannen (1984b) finds that interactants who do not share the contextualization conventions of New York Jewish speakers of English often evaluate them as intrusive, overbearing, and abrupt. One particular feature she examines is called the "machine-gun question," a direct, high pitched, fast-paced way of questioning with reduced syntactic form. Tannen (1984a) also finds such evaluations with other conversational features that comprise the New York Jewish "high-involvement" style. Through extensive analysis of intracultural and cross-cultural interaction, she demonstrates that such negative evaluations actually occur because cross-cultural interactants express involvement and considerateness in different ways. Thus, contextualization conventions that are meaningful intraculturally are misinterpreted cross-culturally.

It is one thing to know that there are differences in contextualization conventions across groups, another thing to be able to recognize them, and yet another thing to know when our own cultural interpreting processes are at work in evaluating the other group. Even those who are highly aware of cross-cultural differences often have difficulty in realizing that they are judging others with their own yardstick. I encountered this form of cultural blindness when I participated in a workshop for American EFL teachers going to Japan. As presenters in the workshop, our objective was to prepare the teachers for cross-cultural problems that they might experience generally in Japan, and specifically with their students, intermediate to advanced Japanese learners of English at the postsecondary school level. In our brainstorming session, we had chosen the areas for presentation, and we began distributing a list of these areas to presenters. In discussing who would be responsible for the "writing" section, one American ESL workshop instructor volunteered, saying she had had much experience in correcting Japanese student writing. I asked her if she was going to demonstrate differences in the rhetorical practices of American and Japanese expository style. She responded with, "No I don't think I'll talk about that—it's not really that important. I *know* Japanese always write off the topic. They just have to learn to write correctly. All that other stuff will come." Although I did not ask her directly, in the conversation that followed, I was able to elicit her opinion of what "writing correctly" is: writing grammatically.

This conversation was interesting on two levels. First, despite her expertise in ESL instruction, she considered "grammar" to be the most important aspect of writing for intermediate and advanced foreign learners of English. Once you get the grammar right, everything else follows. As discussed earlier, foreign language learners often experience difficulties resulting from crosslinguistic differences beyond the grammatical level. In my own experience, as well as in my observation of criticisms directed at other Japanese authors writing in English, the primary criticism seems to be at the level of rhetoric, not grammar. Although organization in writing is not transferrable across languages, writers often (unconsciously) transfer such practices. When this happens, readers cannot make sense of such writing, and therefore, evaluate the nonnative writer as disorganized. Thus, rhetorical style *is* important; in addition to grammar, foreign students also need to learn a cultural writing style.

My conversation with the workshop presenter is also interesting on another level. She dismissed rhetorical style differences as unimportant because Japanese students always write off-topic. However, that is precisely why it is important: Japanese students write what seems to American English readers as off-topic because it makes sense in Japanese; it is an institutionalized rhetorical practice. Hinds' (1983) contrastive study shows such a difference in American and Japanese rhetorical style. Japanese rhetorical style has a feature "*ten*" (the point that is not directly related to the main theme) which is obligatory in the organizational structure of Japanese writing, as shown below.

A.	ki	First, begin one's argument.
B.	sho	Next, develop that.
C.	ten	At that point where this development is finished, turn the idea to a subtheme where there is a connection, but not a directly connected association (to the major theme).
D.	ketsu	Last, bring all of this together and reach a conclusion. (Hinds, 1983, p. 188)

The organizational structure in Japanese rhetorical style therefore deliberately includes the introduction of a point that is not directly related to the main theme; it is a style that is both institutionalized and appropriate in Japanese expository writing (Hinds, 1983; Odlin, 1989). Japanese often use the "*ten*" when writing in English, but because this is not a feature in the organizational structure of writing in American English, American readers often judge Japanese writing as "off-topic." In turn, unawareness of specific differences in contextualization conventions leads to stereotypes: Japanese are always writing (and talking) about things off-the-topic, they don't get to the point, they are *evasive*.

In short, limiting foreign language learning to the confines of grammar creates a highly defensive group of learners (which seems to be the result of such stereotypes on the Japanese-learner end). Instead, cross-cultural interactants need to know about specific differences in one another's contextualization conventions. Such insights allow members of cross-cultural groups to recognize "what's going on" in cross-cultural interaction, when their own conventions are being transferred, why others evaluate them in the way they do.

The Cross-Talk model has significant applied value, as it was originally aimed at helping cross-cultural interactants discover why they felt negatively about each other. I have already drifted across the boundary in discussing theory to illustrating its application. In its application, I discussed the consequences of overlooking differences in contextualization conventions: mutual negative sentiments and stereotypes. Although the kind of ill feelings harbored in the American-Japanese situation described above may not have serious repercussions, in other situations, the outcome may be more grave.

For example, in Gumperz's (1982b) study of a courtoom case, a Filipino physician on duty in an emergency room of a U.S. Navy Hospital in Southern California is indicted for perjury. The incident concerns a child who comes to his care in the emergency room, allegedly suffering from sunburns. Initially, the Filipino physician diagnoses the child as suffering from first and second degree sunburns, a diagnosis that collaborates the story of the child's parents. At this point, the child is released from the hospital, but brought back several hours later, then diagnosed by another physician as having third degree burns and suffering from severe dehydration. This time, the child is sent to a burn center at a civilian hospital; however, he dies on the way.

In a series of subsequent trials, first, the child's stepfather is convicted with second degree manslaughter as it becomes evident that he intentionally inflicted burns upon the child. In this trial, the Filipino physician testifies against the child's stepfather, thus implicitly indicating that he had suspected child abuse on the patient's first visit to the emergency room.

However, verbally, he testifies to the contrary. The physician is then indicted for perjury with the prosecution claiming that his testimony conflicts with the FBI report. As the defense noticed the physician's "funny" use of grammar, Gumperz's analysis (1982b) and expert witness testimony showed that the physician had a misleadingly nativelike command of English in his pronunciation and grammar, but that he also had certain "grammatical oddities." These oddities were actually contextualization cues that reflected the organizational structure of Tagalog and Aklan discourse, the physician's native languages. The Filipino physician's trial caused great public concern as it exacerbated the existing racial tension between the Filipinos and the white suburban communities in the Southern Californian region. Thus, Gumperz (1982b) shows that differences in discourse strategies often have serious and sometimes traumatic repercussions beyond the personal level.

Method

The Cross-Talk Model is also noteworthy for its "interpretive" and "comparative" method. I discuss each of these apsects of the method, as they are the frequently misunderstood contextualization conventions of interactional sociolinguistics. "Interpretive" studies make some linguists nervous. Such linguists usually denounce interpretive studies as "particularistic" and "subjective." This uneasiness occurs in part because interpretive studies typically rely more heavily on qualitative techniques rather than quantitative. Studies using quantitative techniques are often thought to produce more "rigorous" and "scientific" results that prove something. However, there are a few misconceptions in this line of thinking. First, the philospher Whitehead (1978) discusses the mistaken significance placed on the abstract, rather than the actual as the "fallacy of the misplaced concreteness." Second, there are many ways of examining an interaction. Thus, as is true of cultural varieties of conversational strategies, there is no single "right way" for interactional analysis, but different and multiple ways of understanding participant behavior in interaction. Below, I explain each of these "fallacies" in further detail.

To begin with, what is real in interactions is the "subjective" experience of the participants in the interaction. As Bateson (1979) argues, there is no such thing as an objective experience;

Experience is always subjective. The purpose of investigating interactions is, then, to make sense of a subjective experience. A qualitative approach is one way in which such understanding is interpreted. In this sense, all studies of human interactions are "interpretive" because whether or not interactional data are quantified, they are always interpreted. Quantified data are often seen as "noninterpretive" because there is a tendency to think that the quantification is the focus of study. It is easy to forget that it is the interaction that is the subject of study, not the quantification. Quantification is a technique from which an analyst interprets results; it does not speak for itself. Thus, quantified and non-quantified empirical data both involve interpretation.

Furthermore, the questions asked about sociocultural interaction are different from those asked in the physical sciences. A difference, however, does not mean that they are invalid or inferior; they are significant in their own right, but on different terms. The sociologist Max Weber (1968) makes this point repeatedly.

> We can accomplish something which is never attainable in the natural sciences, namely the subjective understanding of the action of the component individuals. The natural sciences on the other hand cannot do this, being limited to the formulation of causal uniformities in objects and events and the explanation of individual facts by applying them. We do not "understand" the behavior of cells, but can only observe the relevant functional relationships and generalize on the basis of these observations. This additional achievement of explanation by interpretive understanding, as distinguished from external observation is of course attained only at a price—the more hypothetical and fragmentary character of its results. Nevertheless subjective understanding is the specific characteristic of sociological knowledge. (Weber, 1968, p. 1:15)

In short, social questions are different from physical ones, and social data require interpretation.

There is also the question about the interpreter: How can an interaction be described objectively if it is interpreted? Again, as Bateson (1978) points out, there is no objective experience, including those of the interpreter's. In any analysis of interaction, the observer is always part of the subjective experience. However, as Tannen (1984a) explains, interpretations need not be erratic. An analyst interprets systematically recurring interactional phenomena in empirical data.

Another question that is often raised is about the "generalizability" of interpreted data. This question is asked because interpretive studies are frequently case studies. Findings from case studies are not "generalizable" in the statistical sense, as in "generalizable to a larger population given a confidence level or 95% or above, with little standard deviation." This is because understanding in a interactional context cannot be measured with or without confidence levels; meaning occurs in a "particular" context (Becker, 1988). Such a response usually provokes more apprehension because nonquantifiability often translates into an inability to test the examined question. However, as Bateson (1979) reminds us, no analysis proves anything except in complete abstraction. Rather, through interpretation of empirical data, interactional sociolinguists seek to illustrate systematically recurring patterns in interaction. Such patterns are "demonstrably motivated, not random" (Tannen, 1984a:37). In short, an interpretive approach is both "particularistic" and "subjective," but not in the pejorative sense. It is an approach that makes sense for understanding human interaction.

The "comparative" method has had a long history in sociology (see for example, Mill, 1859; Przeworski and Teune, 1970; Smelser, 1976), and has recently received attention in a range of subdisciplines in sociolinguistics: in variation theory (Labov, 1972), in ethnography of speaking (Hymes, 1962), and in interactional sociolinguisticts (Gumperz, 1982a; Tannen, 1984a). Despite the variety of techniques used in these subdisciplines, the comparative method is used in all sociolinguistic analyses to examine linguistic factors in combination with social forces. Because sociolinguistic comparison includes aggregate social data, or linguistic phenomena beyond the level of a sentence, it differs from the traditional approach of comparison in American linguistics, known as Contrastive Analysis (Lado, 1957), or from the method used in Europe, known as Contrastive Linguistics (Fisiak, 1980). Contrastive Analysis contrasts first language (L1) and second language (L2) phonemic or grammatical forms to predict the degree of difficulty L1 language learners might have with the L2 target language; Contrastive Linguistics (Fisiak, 1980) seeks to improve theories of grammar by contrasting different grammatical features in several languages. In contrast to these methods, sociolinguistic analyses examine how meaning is derived from patterns in structural and cultural contexts by means of comparison. This then allows us to understand the sociolinguistic similarities shared within a group, as well as the differences across groups.

The comparative method is also important because it mirrors the kind of understanding that goes on in an interaction. When participants use interpretive frames, they compare "what is going on in the interaction" with past experience. Thus, we often understand through comparative interpretation. The "interpretive" and "comparative" aspects of the Cross-Talk model are therefore assets to the method of understanding face-to-face interaction. They reflect how participants compare past experience with the ongoing interaction to interperet the meaningfulness in their particular and subjective experience.

In short, the Cross-Talk model contributes to the theoretical framework of interactional sociolinguistics in the following ways. First, it offers a way to study and understand the relationship between conversational strategies and underlying cultural expectations. Second, Cross-Talk characterizes how cross-cultural interactants use different conversational strategies to reflect their varied interactional assumptions about interaction.

MOTIVATING FORCES: INTERACTIONAL CONTEXT

Grounded in the theoretical framework of interactional sociolinguistics and guided by the Cross-Talk model, in this study, I compare American and Japanese topic-management strategies in business meetings. In light of the interactional contexts discussed previously (culture, encounter, and conversation), in the following section, I discuss several motivating forces that directed the focus of this particular investigation.

At the most general level, my motivation for the study derives from an applied goal: a comparison of conversational strategies and cultural assumptions may help uncover plausible sources for cross-cultural stereotyping. Moreover, because it is important to understand the conversational strategies and the cultural context that is meaningful to each group, both American and Japanese conversations must be valued in their native contexts before cross-cultural comparisons can be made. Although the literature in the study of Japanese conversation continues to grow (for example, Clancy, 1972, 1982; Hinds,

1978a, 1978b, 1980; Hinds & Hinds, 1979; LoCastro, 1987; Y. Matsumoto, 1988; S. Maynard, 1983, 1989; and Tsuda, 1984 have studied various aspects of Japanese conversation; Clancy, 1980; Elzinga, 1978; Hayashi, 1988; and S. Maynard, 1986b, 1989 have compared several conversational American and Japanese features), conversational and cross-cultural research have traditionally focused on interactions where an Indo-European language is the medium of communication. In the present study, then, I first examine the interactions from emic perspectives (an American interaction in English, and a Japanese interaction in Japanese), and then I compare across groups.

Furthermore, since interpretive frames vary according to particular encounters, comparative studies of conversational strategies require the examination of a single type encounter. I focus on the business encounter to compare differences in conversational strategies that occur as a result of specific differences in American and Japanese expectations about business interaction, in addition to general differences in cultural expectations. Thus, by comparing American and Japanese conversation in business meetings, this study contributes to the small but growing body of conversational research in meetings (Atkinson, Cuff, & Lee, 1978; Cuff & Sharrock, 1985) and other formal encounters, such as doctor-patient interaction and medical interviews (Shuy, 1974; Tannen & Wallat, 1987), academic, counseling, job, or "gatekeeping" interviews (Erickson, 1976, 1979; Erickson & Schultz, 1982; Fiksdal, 1986; Mishra, 1982; Scollon & Scollon, 1981; Thorpe, 1983), courtoom and public committee negotiations (Gumperz, 1976, 1982b; Gumperz & Cook-Gumperz, 1982b; Shuy, 1982, 1986) and classrooms (Mehan, 1980; Michaels & Collins, 1984; Philips, 1972; Shultz, Florio, & Erickson, 1982).

Finally, interpretive frames also vary according to a specific conversational context. The focus of comparison in the American and Japanese business conversations is (conversational) topic. In contrast to the widely researched notion of grammatical topic,[3] the intuitive concept of conversational topic has only

---

[3] Studies of grammatical topic typically develop a linguistic typology comparing languages according to how they encode topic-comment relations. For research on grammaticalized topic in Japanese, see for example, Hinds (1986), Kuno (1973), S. Maynard (1981, 1987) and Shibamoto (1984). Japanese grammatically encodes the topic-comment relation in the topic-marker *wa* versus the subject-marker *ga*. However, syntacticians still debate the specific encoding and function of the markers *wa* and *ga* in Japanese.

been recently examined. Moreover, philosophers, pragmaticists, and discourse analysts call conversational topic "discourse topic" (Keenan and Schieffelin, 1975), "episode" (Van Dijk, 1982), "paragraph" (Hinds, 1977, 1978a), "theme" (Danes, 1974; Mathesius, cited in S. Maynard, 1986a; S. Maynard, 1986a), and define it as a formal, bounded, and measurable entity. Following Shuy (1974, 1982, 1986), sociolinguists have not attempted to define "topic" formally, rather, they appeal to a more intuitive gauge that might respond to a nonparticipant's question: "What are you talking about?"

My definition of topic is synonymous with Shuy's. Furthermore, I view topic boundaries, hereafter referred to as "topic margins," as emergent in interaction, available as a possibility as the interaction progresses. In this book, I use the term "margins" as opposed to "boundaries" to emphasize the point that the areas that contain the ending of a previous topic, and the beginning of the next topic are "fuzzy," rather than discrete points located in conversations. Thus, while bounded and organized, I view the concept of conversational topic as primarily intuitive. With culturally salient ways of strategically coordinating conversational data (both linguistic and nonlinguistic) in topics, conversationalists have native strategies for topic management that include an intuitition for appropriate points in which to raise and change topics. In turn, such a command of topics allows interactants to satisfy their cultural expectations for interaction. It is therefore the intuitive sharedness of such topic-management conventions that allow participants to reply on a nonparticipant's question, "What are you talking about?" with "We're talking about [ongoing topic]" or "We were talking about [previous topic], but now we're talking about [on-going topic]."

In identifying the topics for the present study, I began by playing the role of a participant, and responded at the most general level to a nonparticipant's question, "What are you talking about?" Following this preliminary sketch of what Shuy (1986) refers to as a "topic flow" I then checked for contextualization cues (linguistic and nonlinguistic cues in the conversation) in the margins of these intuitively identified topics. In each case, my intuition was corroborated with intraculturally consistent patterns of conversational cues, or what I refer to as "topic-management strategies." Conversationalists therefore use intraculturally meaningful strategies in topic margins to mark and bound intuitively developed topics. Furthermore, interactants do not limit their use of topic-management strategies to margins. Throughout a topic, with strategies for distributing talk and for making points, participants continually manage and organize their conversational topics.

In Chapters 3 through 5, I demonstrate that strategies for topic management are motivated in part by the conversationalists' sociocultural expectations. Similarly, in his analysis of an Italian-American, four-party dinner conversation, Erickson (1982a) illustrates how topical cohesion in the conversation is structured and sustained by its sociocultural context. Erickson characterizes the participants as carefully constructing the conversation, by "making use of constraints provided by the actions of others as structure points around which one's own activity can be shaped" (Erickson, 1982a:44). By examining posture, gaze, listing routines, and rhythmic organization of speech prosody in conjunction with commonplace sources of topical content, Erickson shows how each of these conversational features plays an important role in defining, coordinating, and organizing participants in their rhythmic coconstruction of the multilayered conversation.

Following the pioneering work of Erickson on topical cohesion and its relation to sociocultural variables, this study examines how American and Japanese use a variety of strategies to manage topics and organize themselves within the sociocultural framework of a particular encounter. I therefore examine topic management with a primary focus on interactional use within a sociocultural context, rather than formally investigating topics as disjunct from conversationalists and its multiple interactional contexts. This study therefore contributes to the study of topic management from the perspective of interactional sociolinguistics.

Building further upon Erickson's work, I also investigate American and Japanese topic-management strategies in comparison. A comparative study of topic management is potentially useful, as it illustrates how participants use shared strategies intraculturally, but also how the American and Japanese participants use different strategies across groups. Such a comparison has applied implications as it explores the underlying reasons for potential miscommunications and negative evaluations that may occur in cross-cultural communication. Although shared strategies for topic management create interactional accord, unshared strategies often result in miscommunication and negative evaluations. For example, Tannen's

(1981b) study illustrates that while the strategy of abrupt topic shifting created rapport among speakers of New York Jewish style, it caused problems in communicating with members unfamiliar with the style. Similarly, in their studies of Indian English, Gumperz, Aulakh, and Kaltman (1982) and Mishra (1982) demonstrate how speakers of Indian English use thematic structures that are interpreted as coherent in intracultural communication; however, when used with speakers of Western English, the Indians are often judged as being loose, illogical, and slow. Thus, a study comparing American and Japanese topic-management strategies serves the purpose of understanding one conversational context in which cross-cultural misunderstanding may potentially occur.

In sum, by comparing topic-management strategies in American and Japanese business meetings, my goal is to examine how differences in American and Japanese strategies for topic management reflect differences in their respective expectations about cultural behavior and business interaction. Guided by the theoretical and methodological framework of interactional sociolinguistics, I hope to explore such aspects of American and Japanese sociolinguistic behavior, and thereby shed light on why both groups frequently misunderstand and stereotype one another in cross-cultural communication.

CONCLUSION

In conclusion, I have argued that the concepts of "context," "interpretive frame," and "sharedness" are basic to interactional sociolinguistic theory (Gumperz, 1982a; Tannen, 1984a), and critical for interactional understanding. I then showed how Gumperz, Jupp, and Roberts (1979) built upon the framework of interactional sociolinguistics to arrive at the premise of the Cross-Talk model: Cross-cultural miscommunication occurs because different sociocultural groups use different conversational strategies that reflect differences in their respective expectations about appropriate behavior for interaction. In Chapters 3 through 5, I demonstrate the strategies that American and Japanese officers use to manage topics, and in the following chapter, I examine the respective expectations for interaction that such strategies reflect. By comparing topic-management strategies in business meetings, I hope to show the unique ways in which the American and Japanese officers achieve interactional understanding. Doing so may then allow us to catch a glimpse of what it means to interpret an American and Japanese conversation-in-context—from each respective native's point of view.

CHAPTER 2

INTERACTIONAL EXPECTATIONS: WITHIN-GROUP INDEPENDENCE AND NONCONFRONTATION

In Chapter 1, I presented several key concepts in interactional sociolinguistics (Gumperz, 1982a; Tannen, 1984a). One key notion is that participants "understand" the ongoing conversation by relying on past contexts and interpreting through frames. I also presented the premise of the Cross-Talk model (Gumperz, Jupp, & Roberts, 1979): Conversational strategies reflect cultural expectations about interaction. Thus, the dynamics of conversation involve a process of understanding "past contexts" and the expectations that grow out of their experience.

This chapter compares several aspects of past contexts on which Americans and Japanese base their interpretive frames of expectation. I compare these contexts in two spheres of interaction introduced in Chapter 1: the context of culture, and the context of encounter. Both these interactive spheres influence the context of conversation so that different expectations about cultural interaction in general, and business interaction specifically, guide Americans and Japanese to use different strategies of conversation and topic management in meetings. These comparisons are not exhaustive, but rather illustrative of the most prominent aspects of the cultural and business-related expectations reflected in American and Japanese topic management. I begin by comparing two key cultural dimensions, and then highlight differences in the business encounter.

INTERACTIVE EXPECTATIONS

In the following section, I compare American and Japanese expectations for interaction along two continua: the Individual-Group Dimension and the Talk-Silence Dimension. In the continua of these relative dimensions, I argue that Americans prefer the interactional modes of individuality and talk, but Japanese prefer the modes of group and silence. Figure 2-1 illustrates the relative positions of Americans and Japanese in the continua of these two dimensions.

THE INDIVIDUAL AND THE GROUP

> Americans are like peas on a plate, Japanese, like rice in a bowl. (Wagatsuma, 1985)

Following Althen (1988), Carbaugh (1988), Fallows (1989), and Polanyi (1989), I begin by arguing that Americans see themselves as "individuals" who preserve their "rights," make "independent choices," are "honest" and "responsible for their own actions," and expect to be "respected" for practicing these symbols through a sociopolitical "contract." In contrast, I argue with Cathcart and Cathcart (1982), Lebra (1986), Moeran

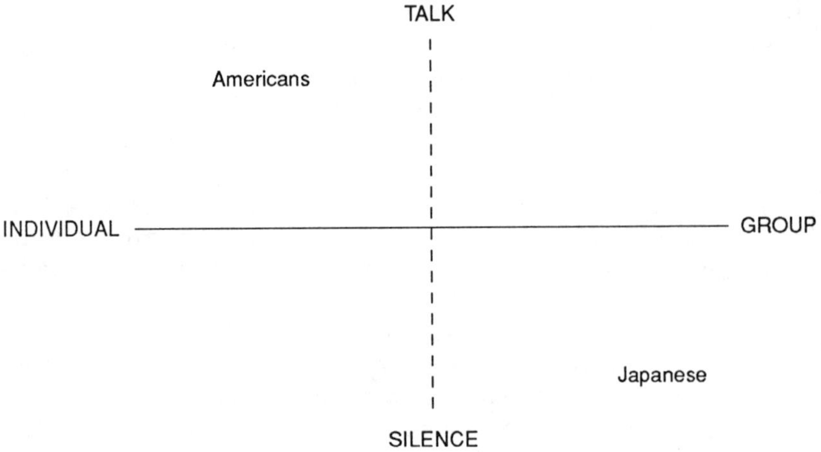

FIGURE 2.1. AMERICAN AND JAPANESE EXPECTATIONS

(1986), Nakane (1970, 1986) and Namiki and Sethi (1988) that Japanese identify themselves as members of a "group" that tries to preserve "*wa*" (harmony) through interdependent, emotional ties, or what Doi (1971, 1982, 1986), Haga (1985), Kondo (1990) and McCreary (1986) have discussed as the concept of "*amae*." I then discuss the American preference for, but the Japanese distrust of, talk. Finally, I show that the two dimensions (individuality and talk for Americans, and collectivity and silence for Japanese), interact complimentarily for the most part, but also present both Americans and Japanese with what Bateson (1979) has called a "double bind." The internal conflicts then produce different interactive expectations for each group: Americans expect "within-group independence," but Japanese, "nonconfrontation."

The American Individual

In his study of American talk in *Donahue*, Carbaugh (1988) describes scene after scene of audience applause following the "proper" portrayal of an American person: an individual. Carbaugh argues that while Americans belong to a range of subclasses (women, gays, senior citizens, etc.), they all belong to the metaclass of individuals. The symbol of an "individual" is therefore important in the heterogeneous American population because it simultaneously distinguishes each American, while uniting all Americans. Thus, each American interaction sets the stage for the questioning and affirmation of the cultural symbol of individuality. In such metaphorical testing, Americans use a unique set of vocabulary to talk about individuality: "rights," "independent choice," "honesty," "respect," and "contract." All of these concepts are described in Carbaugh (1988) and Polanyi (1989) with the exception of the notion of "contract," discussed by Nakane (1970). In the following, I discuss each of these terms in turn.

Each American individual has rights, expresses these rights, and expects others to listen to such requests. Furthermore, rights are distributed equally, hence, "equal rights," and are protected by a contract such as the Bill of Rights, Miranda Rights, Affirmative Action, and so on. When a right is abused, it is equally as important for the abused to "stand up for his or her rights," as it is for others to try to correct the unjustified situation. Thus, rights are a critical criteria for individuality. As summarized by Carbaugh (1988, p. 27):

> To have rights, then is to have individual rights. To express individual rights is to construct a world in terms of the individual.

This expression of individual rights is pervasive in American society; it is applied in every intracultural American encounter, including business. In the next section, I discuss the way in which the American concept of equal rights is used in the American business meeting.

Another attribute of individuality is independent choice. Americans prefer to choose because choice entails the individual "freedom" to choose among options, thus, "freedom of choice." Americans value the freedom to choose because the final decision among alternatives will be "informed." An American who makes an informed decision is, as Polanyi (1989:111) describes, "adjusted, in charge of his life." Furthermore, Americans prefer to choose independently because each individual has the right to make his or her own choice. By making their own choices, Americans take action into their own hands, and determine their own actions. In this way, they are in charge of their decisions as well as their time and space. Conversely, an American who does not make independent choices is not an individual. S/he does not "take charge of his/her life," and is seen as weak, dependent, and incompetent; s/he is "a push-over."

However, individually made and exercised choices and rights have social consequences. As an American individual, making independent choices and standing up for one's rights involves commitment and responsibility for one's own actions. This means that Americans should be able to talk about rights and choices honestly, and respect others for doing the same. In short, because the American contract includes the right to independent choices, different choices must be respected. The American contract therefore encodes a respect for differences among individuals, constructing a sense of individuality unique to the American culture.

To arrive at the notion that the individual is a prominent cultural symbol of America, I began by asking the question, "What makes an American American?" Capturing the essence of any culture is difficult, as is describing the American-ness of Americans. However, outsiders (non-Americans) seem to have less difficulty in describing "Americans" than insiders (Americans). For example, in casual conversations with Japanese and Europeans, these non-Americans answer quite knowingly and matter-of-factly that "An American is someone who has an American passport, someone who is a citizen of America," or that "There is no such thing as an American because there is no such thing as an American culture." Outsiders make such naive remarks because in describing Americans, they must simply make the distinction between themselves and Americans; "Americans are different from us." For Americans, however, the description is about themselves, thus, more problematic. Such problematicity is reflected in their response to the above question; Americans typically respond with retorts such as, "But you can't just say Americans because there are so many different kinds of Americans."

It is true that there are many different kinds of Americans. In my study, the three participants in the American meeting belong to one kind of group: American citizens of Northwestern European ancestry; two women and one man. I discuss this group again in the next section on business expectations. While recognizing that there are "different kinds of Americans," here I have argued that there is an "American" culture which goes beyond the differences of gender, race, or creed. It consists of "Americans" who are united under the common cultural symbol of individuality. Furthermore, because I compare two national groups, my comparison is between groups, rather than between subclasses. The emphasis of my study on cross-group comparisons stems from an interest in examining the cultural symbols with which all members of a group, Americans or Japanese, identify. Thus, while I recognize the American metamessage, "Don't just lump us all together, we're not all the same," the focus of my study is different.

My main point, then, is that American culture is composed of symbols, among which the most prominent is the individual. Americans are individuals who fight for their own rights, and preserve the rights of others, make independent choices, and are earnest and responsible for their own actions. Americans respect these attributes of individuality in other Americans, and in turn, expect to be respected. Such respect is upheld by a sociopolitical contract of rights and choices.

The Japanese Group

In contrast to the American individual, one of the most prominent symbols in Japanese culture is the group. As the anthropologist Nakane (1970, p. 120) explains, "This [Japanese] society gives precedence to the institutional system over individual quality." A single person is, therefore, only an incomplete part of the group; a place-holder which Lebra (1986:67) calls a "*bun*-holder." *Bun* means "portion," "share," "part," or "fraction," thus, a Japanese group member or *bun*-holder is merely "conceived as a fraction" (Lebra, 1986, p. 67). An American individual has rights and choices, but a Japanese *bun*-holder has a place in a group.

Lebra (1986, p. 68) also points out that all "*bun*-holders are interdependent." This Japanese need for mutual dependency not only opposes the American notion of "independent choice," but also emphasizes a difference in relationship among American individuals, and among Japanese *bun*-holders. That is, Americans resolve differences among individuals by invoking a "contract" which says, "Each individual has a right to his/her independent choice." As a group, Americans must respect that contract. For Japanese, there are no such differences between *bun*-holders because they are part of the same group. Thus, there is no need for a contract to resolve individual differences. Rather, Nakane (1970) maintains that *bun*-holders work closely and solely for the sake of the collective group, and the relationship of *bun*-holders is characterized by strong, loyal, and nonrational emotional ties.

In Japanese, this relationship of emotional interdependency is known as *amae*, a concept which Doi (1971, 1982, 1986) has analyzed in great detail. The word *amae*, the reciprocal feeling of nurturing concern for and dependence on another, comes from the verb *amaeru*. Doi (1986, p. 121) defines *amae* from the point of view of the beneficiary as "to depend and presume upon another's benevolence." As Kondo (1990) explains, when the beneficiary receives too much *amae*, it results in the dependent's *wagamama*—an overindulgence in the *amae*, and an expectation that one should receive more than his/her share of *amae*. On the part of the benefactor, too little *amae* is negligence too much, spoiling (this point of view is generated from the verb *amayakasu*, to spoil). As Haga (1985) and other scholars of Japanese behavior have argued, the right balance of *amae* in a relationship, on the other hand, leads to a permissive interdependence between a kind of protector and protected; it maintains the *wa*, the harmonious integration of the collective group.

Doi (1986) points out that a similar concept exists in the West, but that it is often repressed. This is because such dependency on others goes against the American value of the "individual"; Polanyi (1989) citing Greenwald explains that Americans view dependent persons as incompetent and weak.

> Warning: Beware of the person who sends the message implicit or explicit, "I want someone to take care of me." Chances are he or she lacks inner intimacy and feelings of stability and self-love. (cited in Polanyi, 1989:133)

For Americans, a strong individual is a better one, someone who can "stand on his/her own two feet"; someone who stands out as an individual. For Japanese, the proverb, "*deru kugi wa utareru*" (the nail that sticks out gets hammered back in) reflects how a group member should not stand out. In fact, translating the compliment in English, "She's a real individual!" to Japanese becomes an insult: "*Kosei no tsuyoi hito ne*!" ("What a person with strong individuality!"). This pejorative remark has the combined sense of: "She's weird (different) and selfish (does what she wants without conforming)." Instead of standing out as an individual, as Haarmann (1989) accurately captures, *bun*-holders want to be *hitonami* (common, average, ordinary).

Young American adults who have had the experience of living in Japan often find the expected *amae* or interdependence to be overbearing and infringing upon one's privacy. For example, in "homestay" situations, my friends have repeatedly complained about their lack of independence and privacy; the end result being that they feel as if they are treated as children by their host parents. The young Japanese American anthropologist, Kondo (1990), writes about her frustration in adjusting to this difference in cultural behavior during her stay in Japan. She describes an incident where her neighbors continually "check up" on her when she is sick. As part of their caretaking, they bring her all kinds of "get well" meals and good will; however, Kondo describes how she feels overcrowded. She would have simply preferred to be left alone. Thus, although the Japanese neighbors intended to convey warmth through their hospitality to Kondo, the degree of nurturing expression far exceeded the level acceptable to an American.

Kondo, however, does appreciate the intentions of the neighbors, and that they accepted her as an *uchi* member, a member of the same group. Acceptance to a group is important among Japanese members as it gives each *bun*-holder the feeling that s/he belongs. Moreover, because the smallest social unit in Japan is the group, each *bun*-holder differentiates his or her behavior in accordance with whether s/he is interacting with members of the same group (*uchi*), or with members of a different group (*soto*).

In an *uchi* encounter, Japanese typically reveal their true feelings (*honne*), but in a *soto* encounter, Japanese only reveal socially accepted views (*tatemae*). Because the participants in the Japanese meeting I examined for the present study have worked for the same company for about twenty years, the meeting is an *uchi* encounter. This meeting is therefore different from a negotiation meeting, which from the point of view of one group, is a *soto* encounter. As Namiki and Sethi (1988, p. 57) point out, in *soto* encounters, or

> when a Japanese faces an outside group, he establishes his point of reference not in terms of who he is but what group he belongs to.

The relationship of group members as organized by the *uchi-soto* relations further differs from the relationship of American individuals in a group. For Americans, the relations among individuals define whether or not the interaction is in-group or out-group, but for Japanese, the context of the encounter defines the *uchi-soto* relations. That is, American individuals have private or public relationships, but the Japanese group has *uchi* or *soto* relationships.

In sum, for Americans, the individual is a prominent cultural symbol, but for Japanese, it is the group. These symbols not only motivate differences in American and Japanese values, but also influence what Americans and Japanese expect from an interaction. In the following, I continue to discuss the different values held by Americans and Japanese by examining another continuum of expectations: talk and silence. Before this discussion, however, I give an example of how the different values placed on the individual and the group can cause a misunderstanding in American-Japanese cross-cultural communication.

This example of cross-cultural miscommunication occurred

in a telephone conversation between myself, a Japanese, and my brother's friend's father, an American (who I call Mr. Brown). From my end, I thought the conversation had a specific goal. My brother and his two male friends needed housing for the coming school year. All three university classmates were finishing their "Junior Year Abroad," and were still overseas. I had been put in charge of finding housing, and had found a townhouse for a group situation that I thought would be acceptable to the three students. However, because I was acting on their behalf, I still needed the consent of the other two parties. I had talked to my own mother concerning my brother, and had also talked with another mother. I had to obtain Mr. Brown's consent before I could put down the deposit to secure the lease. In my mind, it was a simple yes-no option. However, my phone conversation with Mr. Brown seemed to drag on. Each time I would get to a point where I thought I had obtained consent, Mr. Brown would start to ask more questions about the townhouse. After several times of not being able to obtain Mr. Brown's consent, I finally realized what was going on.

At junctures where I thought I had given him enough information about the townhouse I kept asking: "So, I have your consent?" This made him uncomfortable because for Mr. Brown, his son is an individual who must make his own informed decisions. Making a decision on his son's behalf would rob his son of the right to an independent choice. I noticed this after the third time I asked the question, and Mr. Brown responded, "Well, I don't know the area, and when I talked to my son, he seemed to think it would be OK." Because of the interdependent *amae* relationship between parents and children in Japan (found in the family group), parents frequently make decisions for their children no matter how old they are. Thus, it never occurred to me that obtaining Mr. Brown's consent would be any different than obtaining his son's. When I realized this mismatch of expectations, I tried asking, "So your son would think it was all right if I signed the lease for this townhouse?" This strategy worked, and Mr. Brown said, "Yes, I think he would think so." The case was closed. This is a benign cross-cultural misunderstanding that was easily resolved. However, cross-cultural miscommunications often have far more devastating and irreparable consequences. Thus, between Americans and Japanese, how persons are represented is important. Are they individuals or members of a group?

TALK AND SILENCE

The squeaky wheel gets the grease.

Kuchi wa wazawai no moto. (The mouth is the source of calamity)

Another difference between Americans and Japanese is the value placed on talk and silence, respectively. The Talk-Silence Dimension has been studied less frequently than the Individual-Group Dimension. Still, there are comparative studies that indirectly refer to the American preference for, and the Japanese distrust of, talk.[1] For example, Mizutani (1979:67) compares a scene from the original Japanese movie, *The Seven Samurai*, and the adapted American western, *The Magnificent Seven* to illustrate how Americans use talk in a context where Japanese use silence. In both movies, bandits attack a village, and the seven defenders come to the rescue. However, whereas the bandits attack the village in *The Seven Samurai* without verbal warning, in *The Magnificent Seven* the attackers and defenders face each other at the entrance to the town, and one of the defenders asks, "So you want to fight?"

Mizutani's example points not only to the variable uses of talk and silence, but also to what such variability reflects about American and Japanese expectations. In the Japanese version of the movie, a group of defenders protect the village against a group of bandits in silence. This illustrates the Japanese preference for group-to-group interaction, as well as their assumption of silence in the encounter. Thus, while studies of conversation in Indo-European languages often assume that talk is a commodity that is universally valued, Mizutani shows that for

---

[1]Recently, I have noticed that the antithetical weights placed upon talk and silence by Americans and Japanese can be expanded by adding writing to the continuum, creating the continuum silence-talk-writing. For Americans, reliability increases from left to right, talk is more reliable than silence, but writing is more reliable than talk. For Japanese, the contrary is true. Reliability decreases from left to right. Thus, talk is less reliable than silence, but writing is still less reliable than talk.

Graham and Sano (reported in Pfeiffer, 1988:152) point to the American emphasis placed on the written contract, as they advise Japanese business negotiators: "But we arrive at trust primarily through personal relationships, while they rely on lawyers to write tight contracts and settle disputes. We strongly recommend American-style written contracts with Japanese jurisdiction. The written contract is your only assurance of complicance."

Japanese, silence in context is meaningful and valued, and as Philips (1985) and Saville-Troike (1985) also point out, often expected in some non-Indo-European interactions.

In contrast, in the American version, an individual defender asks the question, "So you want to fight?" Although in the end, the bandits indulge the defenders and fighting ensues, in theory at least, the bandits have the right to choose whether or not to answer, and whether or not to fight. Thus, the fact that the defender asks this question indicates his honor of the American symbol of individuality. In the following, I discuss the American preference for talk, and how talk relates to the individual; I then discuss the Japanese preference for silence, and its relation to the group.

American Talk

Given the earlier discussion that Americans have "rights" and "choices," here I discuss how Americans choose talk to express their right to an opinion. Americans use talk to express themselves, and feel that talk "accomplishes" something. Talk is therefore productive, and everyone wants a part of that productivity. This general sentiment about the value and usefulness of talk is so profoundly ingrained in the American culture that it is often assumed. For example, part of Edelsky's (1981:401) definition of a conversational "floor" is: "the right to be heard."

In American interaction, the individual and talk are intricately intertwined. That is, previously I argued that America is composed of individuals, and each individual makes independent choices. This means that there will be many people who have made a number of different choices, making interactions intrinsically problematic. However, I also argued that Americans expect that differences will be respected. To honor such differences, then, Americans use talk to sort out, solve, and work through their problems; talk is a means for mutual understanding. In intimate relationships, talk is seen as not only useful but necessary. For example, as shown in the excerpts below, participants in *Donahue* (Carbaugh, 1988) praised the value of talk, apparently used synonymously with "communication" in maintaining relationships.

> In any relationship you have to communicate. That's the most important part of a relationship and you've got to talk about

> things. I've been married 3 years and I clean the house, I go to the grocery store with my wife and that's the way it should be. She works and she makes more than I do at times and it's no big deal to me but you have to communicate.
>
> The only thing that saved Craig and me is the communication. That's the only thing that helped us. The husband replied: I think that's the key, communication. The wife: If you don't talk it will never work. (Carbaugh, 1988:155-56)

Thus, talk is seen as a means for accomplishing understanding. Bowers (1988, p. 17) further points to the American view that talk is not only "effective," but that its effectiveness can be manipulated.

> There is an underlying assumption that the source can manipulate a number of variables to improve the effectiveness of communication. Teachers, lawyers, and business people all receive specialized training in how to manipulate such variables.

On the other hand, Scollon (1985:21) informs us that Americans view silence as "an absence of communication" and Carbaugh (1988) characterizes silences as seen as "a breakdown in communication." While an American has the right to exercise silence, "opening up" through talk is viewed more favorably, and a silent individual is perceived as "closed" and "uncooperative." As Polanyi (1989:135) summarizes: "If there are problems or upsets among two or more friends, it may become imperative for all involved to have a talk to try to reach an understanding." In short, Carbaugh (1988:67) captures the viewpoint held among mainstream Americans that "those who are silent are suspect," while those who talk are seen as making an honest, open-ended effort in coming to a better understanding of others. For Americans, then, talk expresses individuality, but it also unites. This high regard of talk among Americans most likely originates from Western philosophy. As Thomas Mann once said:

> Speech is civilization itself. The word, even the most contradictory word, preserves contact—it is silence which isolates.

Japanese Silence

Japanese prefer the interactional mode of silence because of the belief that silence best preserves the *wa* (harmony) of the group.[2] In contrast, Barnlund (1975), De Mente (1989), Doi (1982), Hall and Hall (1987), Lebra (1987), M. Matsumoto (1988), Mizutani (1979), and Nakane (1970) inform us that Japanese view talk unfavorably. First, as reflected in the following proverbs discussed in Lebra (1987:345-6), talk gets you in trouble.

tori mo nakaneba utaremaji
(If the bird had not sung, it would not have been shot)

kuchi ni mitsu ari, hara ni ken ari
(Honey in the mouth, a dagger in the belly)

Furthermore, although Americans judge those who can express their thoughts and opinions articulately as "eloquent," Barnlund (1975:164) notes that Japanese view "articulate persons" as "foolish or even dangerous." Japanese are therefore often surprised, if not "put off" by what appears to be the excessive talk of Americans; Japanese perceive Americans as "overly talkative." For example, Doi (1982) recounts a perturbing experience of what seemed to him an exorbitant amount of talk during his participation in an American meal. The contrary is also true; Americans are often frustrated by the so-called "enigmatic," "reticent," or "silent" Japanese.

On the other hand, Lebra (1987) points out that Japanese do not evaluate halting styles negatively, even if those who use such styles occupy prominent positions in the government or business community. Such variant evaluations of the "eloquent speaker" occur because Americans and Japanese have different perspectives of "honesty." As discussed earlier, Americans view those who can "open up" through talk as being honest, but Japanese view talk as unable to capture honest feelings. Another proverb in Lebra (1987) reflects this Japanese point of view: *bigen shin narazu* (Beautiful speech lacks sincerity).

The Japanese preference for silence leads to an explicit and idealized form of "communication" called *haragei* (belly art). Essentially, *haragei* is "silent communication," which results from the Japanese belief that one's feelings cannot be expressed through talk. In more implicit forms, the Japanese preference for a silent mode of communication leads to a repression of explicit talk, where much is left unsaid. Hall and Hall (1987)

---

[2] Saville-Troike (1985) also notes that Japanese authors incorporate "silence" in writing through the use of "...".

characterize this ambiguous and implicit talk as "high-context," as the talk depends heavily on the context of interaction. Ikegami (1989:264-5) likens such "heavy dependence on context" to "child language or poetic language" in Western languages.

High-context talk produces a conversation with numerous intermittent silences or *ma* (space) and filled pauses—one which lacks a clear focus or goal. Nakane (1970) describes the resultant quality of such talk as meandering, and difficult to follow.

> parties to a conversation follow parallel lines, winding in circles and ending up by long descriptive accounts, the narration of personal experiences or the statement of an attitude towards a person or an event in definitive and subjective terms unlikely to invite, or to reach, a compromise. (Nakane, 1970:34-5)

This unfocused and fragmented quality of Japanese conversation appears to be prevalent particularly when participants in a conversation are of more or less equal status (as are the participants in my study). Nakane (1970) describes a contrary situation when the statuses of the participants are unequal; the result is a kind of one-sided sermon on the part of the superior.

In pointing to the fragmented and unfocused nature of Japanese talk, Nakane (1970:125) also notes the sociolinguistic characteristic of sentence incompletion in Japanese.

> a sentence is never completed; the conversation may jump from one topic to another with no apparent linking theme; topics will be taken up at whim of each speaker and in such rapid succession that an outsider may well be unable to catch even the general drift.

Harris and Morgan (1987) also warn American business negotiators that Japanese seldom complete their sentences. Sentence incompletion, which produces the unfocused and fragmented quality of Japanese conversation, is therefore seen as problematic for Americans in cross-cultural negotiations.

Japanese therefore prefer to say less, and depend heavily on the context to convey, interpret, and disambiguate conversational meaning. Doi (1982) explains that this characteristic of Japanese conversations makes individual talk ownership, as well as talk itself, ambiguous. Such ambiguity in Japanese conversation gives precedence to group interaction because unlike American individuals who take the responsibility for their own talk, no one group member takes the responsibility for the negatively viewed talk in Japanese interaction. Thus, the Japanese preference for silence rather than talk compliments the priority placed upon the group.

Moreover, there is a prevalent attitude that it is not what is actually said that is important. This perspective is so pervasive among Japanese that a counselor, Tazuko Shibusawa reportedly uses art therapy with her patients to capitalize on the Japanese emphasis on what is not said. According to Millard's (1990:22) report, Shibusawa perceives art therapy as a better way for Japanese to connect with their emotions than talk. Lebra (1987:346) also discusses the perspective that talk is unimportant with the following proverbs:

Aho no hanashi gui
A fool eats (believes) whatever is said.

Hanashi hanbun
Believe only half of what you hear.

Rather, what is important for Japanese is that communication proceed in an unobtrusive and prescribed way. For example, in his ethnography of a dinner entertainment in Japan, Befu (1986:111) shows that Japanese "face-to-face interaction is like a drama, in which each actor knows what the others are supposed to say." In another example, Kondo (1990) recounts her experience in an "Ethics School" ("*Rinri Gakuen*") in Japan, a school designed to promote cooperation and perseverence among workers. She describes one session in a "Morning Meeting" ("*Asa no Tsudoi*") where participants were asked to deliver speeches. Here she notes that the content mattered less than adherence to a prescribed form. Thus, both Befu's and Kondo's examples demonstrate how Japanese deemphasize talk-content, emphasize structural form, and thereby avoid uncertainty. This Japanese orientation toward talk and interaction seems to account in part for the high frequency of formulaic expressions in Japanese.

In short, in Japanese interaction, everyone knows what others are going to do and say, and as Lebra and Lebra (1986:105) characterize: "actors perform their parts flawlessly according to an unwritten but well-understood script." By rigorously defining the structure of interactional talk, a single individual need not stand out as everyone talks and behaves using the same organizing principles.

By refocusing the attention away from talk and to group interaction, Japanese believe that they can strengthen the group's emotional attachment, and thus better enjoy each other's company. Thus, Nakane (1970:125) stresses the point that it is the ease of personal exchange and the expression of emotionality which Japanese tend to focus upon, rather than understanding individual viewpoints held in a conversation.

> The essence of pleasure in conversation for the Japanese is not in discussion (a logical game) but in emotional exchange; it is not easy for those who have different ideas and backgrounds to join profitably or successfully in such an exercise.

In sum, because talk is viewed negatively, the focus of Japanese conversation is away from talk, and toward the silence that embodies the sharedness of the emotional experience in interaction. This focus is, as Neal Norrick (personal communication, 11/9/89) pointed out to me, one that stresses contact (nonphysical) over content. Further, because Japanese feel that sharedness is best found in low-content/high-context talk and interaction, they prefer conversations that are noncontroversial.

In a recent interaction with an older, Japanese male visiting professor of international relations, I observed an instance of the Japanese emphasis of contact over content. The interaction took place in a university, where I had just finished the "lecture" part of a job interview. The atmosphere had been fairly serious, and as I was waiting for my next interview in the hallway, the Japanese professor invited me into his office saying, "*aa otsukaresama deshita. ne, chotto tsumaranai hanashi o shimashoo yo*" ("Good job. [forumlaic expression] Listen, let's talk about something boring"). I felt a relief with this comment, as I interpreted what he said to mean something further like, "I know you're tired of arguing all these academic points. You've been in the conference room for two hours now, and I know you want to talk about trivial things." And so we did, talking about family, overseas experiences, and so forth.

This interaction was interesting because it showed the professor's knowledge about the Japanese expectation for interaction. That is, talk in unmarked Japanese interaction is nonsurprising or in his words, "boring" ("*tsumaranai*")—void of explicit argumentation and discussions on "interesting" topics which might be characterized as typically Western. Moreover, the professor also showed his expectation of Japanese interaction through an appeal to a Japanese value called *sasshi* (surmise). Examined by Ishii (1984) and Okazaki (1990) among others, *sasshi* is the belief that one can understand thoughts and feelings through virtually silent communication (with very little said); It presupposes active listener interpretation of heavily context-dependent talk. Thus, while all the professor said was, "Let's talk about something boring," he assumed that I would interpret the intended *omoiyari* (empathy), that he was sympathetic to my situation. (*Omoiyari* is a virtue of a superior critical in the Japanese hierarchical dependence structure.) Thus, the professor capitalized on our shared cultural expectation for talk and *sasshi*, and was able to realize the Japanese proverb, *ichi o ieba juu ga wakaru* (Make one point and get ten points across). In doing so, he worked toward fulfilling the Japanese expectation for saying little and maintaining the *wa* in our encounter.

In sum, in Japanese conversation, what counts is not what you say, but the feeling that you convey. Furthermore, in contrast to the American point of view, talk is not seen as accomplishing mutual understanding. Instead, by avoiding direct talk, Japanese avoid confrontation. In turn, because avoiding confrontation ensures synchronized and agreeable interaction, it not only promotes security within the group, but it also avoids uncertainty. Thus, as Namiki and Sethi (1988:61) point out:

> Japanese tend to have high uncertainty-avoidance orientation. For example, the practices of lifetime employment and seniority-based wage and promotion are designed to reduce uncertainty in life and promote security. Conflict and competition are avoided, and group concensus and compromise are emphasized.

In cross-cultural communication, the American use of talk to "resolve differences," and the Japanese use of silence to maintain *wa* (harmony) create the opportunity for what Bateson (1972) calls "complimentary schismogenisis." Tannen (1984a:22) explains this concept as "a dynamic in which two interactants exercise clashing behavior, such that each one's behavior drives the other into increasingly exaggerated expressions of the incongruent behavior in a mutually aggravating spiral." This means that when Americans and Japanese experience cross-cultural communication problems, the Americans will use more and more talk to try to resolve the conflict, and the Japanese will use less and less talk to avoid the problem. De Mente (1989) describes a typical situation in American-Japanese business negotiations where the heightened use of Japanese silence occurs. He reports that when problems arise during negotiation sessions:

> Members of the Japanese team will simply stop talking. Some will lean back and close their eyes, as if sleeping. Others will get up and leave the table, returning to their desks or going to the toilet or whatever, without any sign. (De Mente, 1989:125)

While the readers of de Mente's (1989) book may be forewarned, others are misguided; they are simply told to use their own strategies for problem resolution. For example, in Thian (1988:86), an American businessman in Japan is noted as saying, "It's usually a *gaijin* [foreigner]-Japanese problem with employees, but somehow, you work it out." Thian (1988:86) then comments with the following advice:

> The company and its well-being are always more important than daily, petty squabbles, and talking things over is one way to resolve differences.

"Talking things over" is certainly "one way to resolve differences" among Americans; however, because Japanese prefer a silent mode of interaction and view talk negatively, "talking things over" will most likely result in exacerbating the problem at hand. As Americans try to resolve the problem through talk, Japanese may become increasingly reticent; both sides then descend into the aggravated depths of complimentary schismogenisis.

DOUBLE BINDS

When an individual talks, that talk can be attributed to that individual. Silence, on the other hand, cannot be assigned to a single individual; as S. Maynard (1989) and Tannen (1985c) among others have pointed out, silence belongs to all participants present in a conversational encounter. Thus, as I have so far discussed, in one sense, individuality and talk, and collectivity and silence interact complimentarily. However, the two dimensions also present Americans and Japanese with what Bateson (1979) has referred to as a a "double bind," and what Kondo (1990) calls "existential dilemmas." Double binds occur because both poles in a continuum are desirable and necessary, and because interactants are obliged to balance the conflicting poles simultaneously; they must cope with the paradoxical situation.

In the following section, I describe the American and Japanese double binds that result in combined, interactive expectations. I refer to these expectations as "within-group independence" for Americans, and "nonconfrontation" for Japanese. In the subsequent chapters, I argue that differences in American and Japanese topic management reflect the expectation of within-group independence for Americans, but nonconfrontation for Japanese.

For Americans, a double bind occurs because although individuality is stressed, conversationalists still need to relate to one another and be understood. Furthermore, both individuality and collectivity are expressed through talk. Americans must therefore use conversational strategies that respond to the interactional expectation of both individuality and collectivity. I call this interactive expectation, "within-group independence."

In contrast, for Japanese, a double bind occurs because while interactions frequently require talk, talk is viewed as untrustworthy. This means that each occasion of talk creates a situation for an unreliable, mistrustful interaction, which jeopardizes collectivity in the group. Japanese must therefore use conversational strategies that respond to the interactional expectation of using the mistrusted medium of talk in a way that still allows for conversationalists to reach collective goals. In other words, Japanese must use strategies which deemphasize the significance of talk. I call this interactive expectation, "nonconfrontation."

My conceptualization of "nonconfrontation" is somewhat similar to Ishii's (1984) notion of *enryo-sasshi* (modesty-consideration) competence. Okazaki (1990:11) defines *enryo-sasshi* competence as: "the message sender's avoidance of direct expressions of thoughts and feelings (*enryo* "modesty"), and the receiver's sensitivity to the message (*sasshi* "consideration." *Enryo-sasshi* competence is also comparable to Maynard's (1989:31) "social packaging": "a socially motivated act to construct the content of the utterance in such a way as to achieve maximum agreeablness to the recipient." Finally, nonconfrontation is also akin to the concept of *aiwa* (love and harmony), a conceptual attitude which Kondo (1990:105) describes as one of the key attitudes to gaining a "*sunao na kokoro*," "a naive, receptive, sensitive heart."

There are also broad similarities between the interactional expectations of within-group independence and nonconfrontation described above, and what other scholars have termed: involvement/considerateness (Tannen, 1984a), clarity/distance, camaraderie/deference (Lakoff, 1979), presentational/avoidance rituals (Goffman, 1959, 1967), and positive/negative face (Brown and Levinson, 1987). Although mine is most similar to Tannen's conceptualization of involvement versus considerateness, my modes of expectation differ from those listed above in several important ways. First, I do not take the universalist stance that there are fundamental modes of interaction that underlie all cultures. Thus, I argued that while Americans and Japanese both have double binds, their binds are of a different nature; a different combination of cultural principles coalesce to create the American interactive expectation for within-group independence and the Japanese expectation for nonconfrontation.

Another difference is that while the previously mentioned modes of interaction are examined in a context of Indo-European languages, the interactional expectations I describe are observed in a context of one Indo-European language (American English) and one non-Indo-European language (Japanese). While this may seem like a minor difference at first glance, it is important because universalist approaches sometimes misleadingly extend modes of interaction that are significant for one group to another.

For example, Brown and Levinson (1987:63) begin with the assumption that a constructed model person, who is a "wilful fluent speaker of a natural language" is "further endowed with two special properties—rationality and face." Following Aristotle, Brown and Levinson's (1987:69) "rationality" is "practical reasoning—which guarantees inferences from ends or goals to means that will satisfy those ends." Then, following Goffman, Brown and Levinson's (1987:66) notion of "face" includes: "positive face, the consistent self-image of personality" and "negative face, the basic claim to territories, personal preserves, rights to non-distraction." Brown and Levinson (1987) then characterize Japanese as predominantly responding to negative face wants.

However, based on anthropological and sociological findings reported in Doi (1971, 1973), Lebra (1986), Nakane (1967, 1972), as well as on her own analysis of formulaic expressions in Japanese textbooks, Y. Matsumoto (1988) argues that Brown and Levinson's descriptions of "rationality" and "face" are generated from fundamentally Western assumptions. As Western philosophy differs from its Eastern counterpart, there are sharply different underlying principles for interaction between the two. In contrasting the Western version of "face," "the basic claim to territories, personal preserves, rights to non-distraction" (Brown and Levinson, 1987:66), Y. Matsumoto (1988:405) claims:

> What is of paramount concern to a Japanese is not his/her own territory, but the position in relation to others in the group and his/her acceptance by those others.

Thus, as Y. Matsumoto (1988) suggests, Brown and Levinson's (1987) notion of universal face wants, and their prediction that Japanese typically use negative face, fall short. In my comparison of cultural expectations, I therefore stress the significance of understanding each culture in its own right.

EXPECTATIONS FOR BUSINESS INTERACTION

In this book, I compare topic-management strategies used in an intracultural American meeting (conducted in American English) with strategies used in an intracultural Japanese meeting (conducted in Japanese). I obtained permission to tape-record the conversations through a personal contact in each meeting. I chose these meetings because both are examples of standard weekly meetings of middle-management bank officers in two major financial institutions. In the following, I first describe the similarities and differences of the two meetings in the study, and their relationship to American and Japanese expectations for business interaction.

Similarities

My motive for tape-recording these two meetings was because, at first glance, the two meetings seem fairly similar. There are three participants in each meeting, and all are middle-management bank officers who participate in weekly meetings in two major financial institutions. The American meeting consists of two women and one man; to preserve anonymity, I have given them the pseudonyms: Karen (39), Lynn (33), and Craig (25). All participants are American citizens who spent the majority of their life in the East Coast. They are of Northwestern European ancestry; white, Christian, and of an Anglo-Saxon ethnic background, with the exception of Karen, whose ethnic background is partially Portuguese. The Japanese meeting is a middle-management *kachoo-kai* (Vice Presidents' Meeting), with three male participants. The pseudonyms for the participants in the Japanese meeting are: Shimizu (40), Tanaka (39), and Ikeda (37). (Although I use first names for the American pseudonyms, I use last names for the Japanese pseudonyms, as last name use is the more common form of reference for adults in Japan.) All Japanese participants attended major universities in Tokyo, and spent the majority of their life there. Participants in both meetings report having "moved around" on the job.

For both meetings, I asked one participant to supply me with each participant's title, age, gender, place of birth, and region where majority of life was spent. For the Americans, there is a final category, "ethnic background," however, for the Japanese, because of the relative ethnic homogeneity of Japan, "ethnic background" was not profiled. Instead, the final category for the Japanese meeting is "university attended" because the institution one attends is a major distinguishing factor in Japan, and more so than in America. As Chambers and Cummings (1990:8) report:

> Japan is a more centralized society, whether in government, economy or education. Partly for this reason, Japanese eyes focus on a more restricted set of employers as the most attractive places to work, including the central government and the select group of large firms. These employers tend to concentrate their recruitment efforts at a small number of universities, enhancing the attractiveness of these institutions as places for ambitious young people to study. In the United States, good jobs go to graduate of

> the more prestigious colleges and universities, but the linkage is not so tight, or at least it is not perceived as being so tight. Americans are not as homogeneous in their perceptions of preferred employers, and the routes to good jobs tend to be more varied: from college, yes, but also from graduate school or following experience at some other workplace. Top colleges do not have as clear a monopoly on top jobs, and do not loom so high above the rest. Because top colleges do not stand so high in the United States, less competitive colleges possibly do not sit so low.

Because of this difference, then, the last categories differ between the American and Japanese meetings. The ethnographic backgrounds of the participants in the two meetings are profiled in Table 2.1.

Differences

Despite the general similarities between the triadic meetings, there are several important differences that reflect the marked

TABLE 2.1
ETHNOGRAPHIC PROFILES OF THE AMERICAN AND JAPANESE MEETINGS

			American Meeting		
Name/ Title	Age	Gender	Place of Birth	Region Lived Most Years	Ethnic Background
Craig Associate	25	Male	Virginia	Northwest, Mid-West	Anglo-Saxon
Lynn Asst. VP	33	Female	New York	Northeast Mid-West	Anglo-Saxon
Karen VP	39	Female	Portugal	Northeast	Portuguese/ Anglo-Saxon
			The Japanese Meeting		
Name/ Title	Age	Gender	Place of Birth	Region Lived Most Years	University Attended
Ikeda VP	37	Male	Saitama	Kantoo	Tokyo University
Tanaka VP	39	Male	Tokyo	Kantoo	Keio University
Shimizu VP	40	Male	Tottori	Kantoo	Tokyo University

difference in American and Japanese expectations about how to conduct meetings, and more fundamentally, about how to do business. Such differences in expectations create conversations of such completely differing qualities that an American reader who examined the Japanese meeting transcript asked, "Is this a meeting?" The major difference is that in the American meeting, each participant reports on a particular "deal" in rounds. A "deal" is a relevant business item or transaction, for which an officer is singularly responsible; as defined in Cuff and Sharrock's (1985) study of meetings, and Button and Casey's (1988/89) study of topic initiation, a reporting round is a grouped set of topics, in which each participant independently reports on relevant issues according to a predefined agenda for the meeting. The conversational structure in the American meeting, then, is one in which each participant independently raises and concludes their own deals or topics.

By contrast, in the Japanese meeting, each officer does not single-handedly report on a "deal," because as I explain later, each Japanese officer is not singularly assigned to a deal. Instead, because many officers are involved in concensus decision-making, the kind of individual rounds evidenced in the American meeting does not typically occur in a Japanese meeting. Although round structures are reportedly instituted in more progressive, "Americanized" Japanese companies (Ito, personal communication, 9/16/90), such structures are marked, especially in the conservative banking sector. In light of the absence of round structures, then, the resultant conversational structure in the Japanese meeting appears much looser as any participant can raise and contribute to a topic, topics are not verbally concluded, and any participant can bring up the next topic. To an American, such a conversational structure in the Japanese meeting makes the conversation sound "chatty"; it does not carry a businesslike tone. However, as I argue in more detail, what seems unbusinesslike to Americans is business for the Japanese.

The way the American and Japanese participants structure their topics can be explained in terms of the differences in cultural expectations discussed earlier. The American participants express their right to deliver, carry through, and conclude their own deal through talk, but the contract in the form of an agenda guarantees the distribution of talk to all participants. As Cuff and Sharrock (1985:157) note:

> it [the agenda] solves the problem of equalizing opportunites to talk, regardless of the standing or relationships of parties in the organization. It offers to those who might be afraid to talk, a guaranteed opportunity to say what they like; everyone gets a turn.

Thus, through rounds in the agenda, the American participants distribute talk to each and every individual. Such talk distribution assumes that each individual *wants* to talk, and that each officer has something to report on *individually*. Harris and Morgan (1987:389) thus point out that the organization of a meeting through an agenda is based on the fact that "American managers are trained for specific responsibilities"; thus, they abide by the code of a "division of labor." Assigned talk distributions that assume the individuality of task responsibilities therefore support the American expectation of within-group independence.

This American method of distributing talk contrasts sharply with the Japanese; as Harris and Morgan (1987) describe, because Japanese emphasize teamwork, boundaries between individuals are blurred. In his study of reactions of American employees to Japanese management practices, Kume (1985) records the tremendous amount of confusion created by such blurring of individual task boundaries. One American was noted as saying: "You don't specialize in one field. You do everything. You don't have enough time to really learn 100% or even 80% of one different area" (Kume, 1985:240).

In the Japanese meeting of the present study, the officers emphasize the indistinctness of an individual and his independent task boundaries by not having a participant singularly raise, continue or close a "deal" or topic. Furthermore, because talk exposes and distinguishes individuals, the officers do not rely on a contract in the form of a predetermined agenda to distribute talk to each individual. Rather, they depend on established personal ties to draw the focus away from the negatively viewed talk that divides. In this way, Japanese businessmen serve their expectation of nonconfrontation.

Another noteworthy aspect of the agenda is that it *pre*-assigns talk to each of the American officers. This further contrasts with the Japanese meeting; an absence of an agenda means that the particular talk of each member is locally determined. Recalling Philips' (1989) description of the distribution of activities among Warm Springs Indians, the distribution of talk among the Japanese officers is left open-ended; it occurs on-site, during the meeting. By virtue of the agenda, then, the American officers know in advance specifically "who" is going to talk about "what," but the Japanese do not. The institution and noninstitution of the agenda then again help each group satisfy their interactional needs: As the *pre*-assignment of talk helps set each American individual apart in the group; the local distribution of talk helps Japanese group members blur talk boundaries.

Participants therefore have specific expectations about meetings, of which the most pronounced is the American expectation of a contract or an agenda on the one hand, but the Japanese expectation of maintained personal ties on the other. Because a rigorously applied meeting agenda is replaced with personal ties, to Americans, the Japanese meeting appears "casual" rather than "businesslike." In other words, for Americans, the formal structure of the contract is what makes the business encounter appropriately impersonal and "businesslike"; personal relationships are reserved for family and friends. Although Americans may have business associates who are friends, the two are not necessarily synonymous. Thus, as Miss Manners (Martin, 1990) prescribes business protocol:

> In business, being pleasant and efficient, without exposing one's private emotions, is called a professional demeanor.

Similarly, in his study comparing the expectations of German and American managers, Friday (1989) also characterizes the talk in American business encounters as impersonal.

The impersonal, "professional demeanor" is also upheld in Japanese *soto-* (out-group) relations, such as in Tsuda's (1984) comparative study of American and Japanese salesperson-customer interaction, March's (1988) and McCreary's (1986) work on negotiations, and in De Mente's (1989) investigation of Japanese interaction with foreigners. De Mente (1989:138) notes that "Japanese businessmen who do business with foreigners have two modes of operation—a Japanese mode and a foreign mode." This has come to be a source of great resentment among foreigners in Japan. In voicing such resentment, Thian (1988:57) reports that a president of an American company in Japan was noted as saying, "I was tainted by being a *gaijin* [a foreigner]."

In contrast, among *uchi-* (in-group) members, Japanese relationships are built on personal ties. Because *uchi-* business relations are also intensely personal, Harris and Morgan (1987:393) warn American business negotiators: "Cut and dry relationships with business contacts are inadequate and must be supplemented by a social relationship for maximum effect." As Bennet and Ishino (1963), Fruin (1983), Kondo (1990) and Nakane (1970) describe, such personal relationships are sought after largely because Japanese men's closest relationships are developed in their *kaisha* (company), and employee loyalty and dependency on the institution of the *kaisha* is reciprocated through the *kaisha*'s complete caretaking of its employees. This "caretaking," or what Bennet and Ishino (1963) and Fruin (1983) refer to as a paternalistic managerial ideology, extends into employees' homes. The result, as Nakane (1970:10) explains, is that "the point where group or public life ends and where private life begins no longer can be distinguished." This pervasive influence of the *kaisha* on the Japanese society at large is reflected in the two characters *kai* and *sha* which make up the word *kaisha* (company), which when reversed in order, is the word for "society" ("*shakai*"). Thus, as De Mente (1989:36) notes, "In the Japanese context there is no neat separation between business and personal life." Kume (1985) also discusses the absence of a boundary between "personal" and "organizational" lives, and Nakane (1970:3) makes this point repeatedly.

> *Kaisha* [Company] does not mean that individuals are bound by contractual relationships into a corporate enterprise, while still thinking of themselves as separate entities; rather *kaisha* is "my" or "our" company, the community to which one belongs primarily, and which is all important in one's life. Thus in most cases the company provides the whole social existence of a person, and has authority over all aspects of his life; he is deeply emotionally involved in the association. I would not wish to deny that in other societies an employee may have a kind of emotional attachment to the company or his employer; what distinguishes this relation in Japan is the exceedingly high degree of this emotional involvement. It is openly and frequently expressed in speech and behavior in public as well as in private, and such expressions always receive social and moral appreciation and approbation.

In her eloquent ethnography of the "crafting of selves" in a Japanese company, Kondo (1990) further describes the Japanese company as family and the Japanese family as company. As Kondo (1990) and Nakane (1970, 1983) among others note, the absence of a division between personal and business lives occurs in part because the Japanese concept of "*ie*" (household) derives from the structure of a corporate group, a derivation which reverses the American definition of household and corporate organization.

Moreover, as Namiki and Sethi (1988) discuss, relationships in a company may be characterized in terms of the *amae* or mutual dependence relationship discussed earlier, where there is an *oyabun* (the superior) who takes care of his *kobun* (subordinates). In both words, *oyabun* (the superior) and *kobun* (subordinates), the morpheme "*bun*" (part) indicates how each person is "part" of the larger group. When the first morpheme in each word *oya* (parent) and *ko* (child) are combined, they form a new word, "*oyako*" which describes a parent-child relationship. However, Kondo (1990) informs us that this kin relationship also derives from the definition of corporate relationships, *oyagaisha* (parent company) and *kogaisha* (child company). In short, while Americans make a distinction between their personal and business lives, Japanese do not. This is due in part to the fact that the concept of *ie* (household) is based on a structural organization defined by a corporate relationship.

Two processes in Japanese business support the establishment of personal ties that binds group members. These are: the *ringi* system of concensus decision-making (Kume, 1985; Okabe, 1983; Ouchi, 1981), and nontask sounding talk (Graham and Sano, in Pfeiffer, 1988). The *ringi-sei* is a system of unanimous concensus, which Ouchi (1981:38) describes as one where "a formal proposal is written and then circulated from the bottom of the organization to the top." However, long before a proposal (*ringi-sho*) is written, an idea is passed around "behind-the-scenes," often in entertainment settings (Harris and Morgan, 1987), and checked for interest, feasibility, and approval. The primary focus here, as Harris and Morgan (1987:397) point out, is the definition of the question:

> They decide first if there is a need for a decision and what it is all about. The focus is upon what the decision is really about not what it should be.

When it seems likely that the idea is both plausible and acceptable, the proposal is drafted, and circulated through the organization, and everyone affixes their seal to the document. By this time, as well as in subsequent meetings when such ideas are discussed, the decision is often already made and known to employees. A meeting encounter for Japanese, then, becomes a mere stage of formality, and differs sharply from its American counterpart, which uses the meeting setting as the actual locus for the airing of ideas and subsequent decision making.

Harris and Morgan (1987) also point out that Americans and Japanese often make different kinds of decisions. Americans focus on short-term, "minutia," or small decisions, but Japanese examine the "big" question, the decision of which appears to be more the determination of the company philosophy rather than individualized, task-oriented decision making. Thus, embedded in the assumption about business meetings among Americans is that day-to-day decisions should be made in meetings. Moreover, for Americans, because interaction is intrinsically problematic, and talk resolves such problematicity, "talking it out" accomplishes; decisions are reachable through talk. However, because Japanese do not view talk as a decision making tool, the purpose of interaction for Japanese (particularly in *uchi*-relations) is to enjoy each other's company. This is true in business meetings as well as in casual encounters. In fact, depending on how one defines "decision-making," one can say that Japanese never make decisions. Instead, as Nakane (1970:53) describes, " . . . a majority opinion readily emerges." In advising American businessmen in Japan, De Mente (1989:25) warns that:

> quick individually made decisions will not be forthcoming; that all members of the group have the right to ask questions and express opinions, and that, in principle at least, everyone takes part in all final decisions.

As Kume (1985) also suggests, Americans prefer decisions that are quickly and efficiently executed by an individual officer; however, because the Japanese style of decision making requires more space and time for personal relations, Americans are often frustrated in negotiating with the Japanese.

Another difference in Japanese business practice is the significance placed on what Graham (cited in Pfeiffer, 1988) has termed, "nontask sounding." Referred to as *uchiawase*, nontask sounding talk is part of *nemawashi* (literally, "rootbinding"). The talk of *uchiawase* is characterized by a light personal tone, which as Graham notes, is often interpreted by Americans as having the quality of "small talk": "Americans do not understand why nontask-sounding is so important to us [Japanese]. They consider it small talk" (Graham and Sano, reported in Pfeiffer, 1988:152). Similarly, Harris and Morgan (1987:391) also advise American negotiators: "Wait patiently for meetings to move beyond preliminary tea and inconsequential talk." Americans therefore often think of the "chatty" Japanese discourse as unnecessary and irrelevant to the business at hand; they simply want to "get on with it."

For the Japanese, however, this process of building personal relationships through nontask sounding is at the heart of the matter; trustworthy business relations are established on the basis of personal relationships. Thus, Japanese partake in numerous *uchiawase* and *nemawashi* to build personal but "professional" relationships. Naotsuka et al. (1981) reported in Arima (1989:360) explain that this Japanese style of establishing business relationships differs from the American:

> This *nemawashi* differs from Western-style "spadework" in that it involves the emotions more than the intellect and is performed in terms of sympathetic understanding rather than intellectual agreement. Personal slights or grudges are smoothed over, and friendly relations are reaffirmed. (Naotsuka et al., 1981:170-1, reported in Arima, 1989:360)

In the Japanese meeting of the present study, nontask-sounding talk occurs in the first topic. Before turning to what Americans might consider more "businesslike" topics, the Japanese participants partake in an *uchiawase* to establish a congenial environment for interrelationship and discussion. This, as I have argued, is a common and well-practiced aspect of Japanese business meetings. However, because Japanese businessmen "do business" and conduct business meetings in a different way than Americans, activities that are considered "business" by Japanese are dismissed as not being "business" by Americans.

In short, for Americans, Kume (1985) and Namiki and Sethi (1988) point out that the Japanese style of business that uses *ringi-sei* and *nemawashi* makes the negotiation process painfully long and complicated, which De Mente (1989), March (1988), Thian (1988), Tung (1984) and Van Zandt (1970) characterize as frustrating; Americans see such practices as unbusinesslike. On the other hand, the *ringi-sei* and *nemawashi do* serve the goals of Japanese business, as they support the Japanese businessmen's primary need to establish personal ties in work settings.

In addition to the different ways of doing business thus far described, there are also several important differences in the structural organization of financial institutions in Japan and the United States. First, banks occupy a privileged position in Japanese society. Namiki and Sethi (1988) report that they are at the center of industrial clusters so that there are a number of companies who rely on banks as the main source of capital resources. This contrasts with the more decentralized position occupied by banks in the United States. Furthermore, Namiki and Sethi (1988:80) also inform us that *kachoo*, vice presidents, or section heads have the critical and powerful role in all Japanese firms of "bridging the gap between lower and higher levels of management." On the other hand, in American companies, the role of the vice president is more loosely defined, and varies from company to company, and from individual to individual.

Finally, there is one last difference between the two meetings that concerns a difference in American and Japanese expectations about the role of women in business. In the Japanese meeting, there is a notable absence of women, reflecting the social reality that women are not often found in executive bank meetings. To this end, Tannen (1990) informs us that gender style differences play an important role in interaction. But she also points out that women often make adjustments toward the male style of "report talk" (as opposed to the female style of "rapport talk") particularly in business discourse. Thus, because American men and women both use the male, report-talk style in mixed-gender meetings, the difference in style makeup between the American and Japanese groups according to gender may not be as great as it seems on the surface. However, I do recognize that the patterns of topic management found in the Japanese meeting can only be said to represent those used by Japanese men.

Before concluding this section, a short discussion on the note of "equivalence" or "true contrast" is in order. Some scholars have questioned the "purity" of contrast between the American and Japanese meetings in this study. In my view, such "purity" can only be attained in abstract contrasts (for example, between pairs of phonemes or syntactic structures), or in highly prestructured, experimental settings. Experimental settings may provide for valid and reliable "true contrasts" between the linguistic structures of two groups, but at a cost—a major one, the imposition of one group's structure on another. Such an introduction of a nonnative structure then distorts the rhythm and social meaning embedded in natural, intracultural conversation. Thus, I might have introduced women or round structures into the intracultural Japanese meeting to produce a desirable "equivalence" in an experimental setting; this would perhaps have made for a better or "truer contrast" with the American meeting. However, it would also have created a marked, atypical Japanese executive meeting. Thus, although comparing aspects of naturally occurring conversation may be inconvenient because the data do not produce equations that represent one-to-one correlations of goals and expectations between two groups, I chose to collect conversational data as they naturally occurred because the need to understand conversation in a socioculturally relevant way warrants such a method of investigation. Conversational participants create sociolinguistic meaning in a particular interaction, in ways that are meaningful from native and emic perspectives.

In sum, I have argued that Americans and Japanese conduct business in different ways; they have different ways of reaching decisions, and different ways of building business and personal relationships. Furthermore, because of such differences, Americans and Japanese have different expectations of what should take place in a meeting. Specifically, individual American officers expect to make decisions in meetings, and such decision making be regulated by an agenda. Male, *uchi* Japanese members on the other hand, do not use the meeting encounter for decision making, but rather, as a place to reaffirm personal ties.

EXPECTATIONS, NATIVE STRATEGIES, AND CROSS-CULTURAL COMMUNICATION

To explore the implications of using native strategies in cross-cultural communication in Chapters 3 through 5, I use examples from a variety of observed American-Japanese cross-cultural interactions, as well as from two cross-cultural meetings (referred to as "Personnel" and "Corporate Banking," respectively) collected as backup data. Both of these American-Japanese cross-cultural meetings are conducted in English. In the 28-minute Personnel meeting, there are two participants: one American woman, Sarah (40), and one Japanese man, Ito (59). In the Corporate Banking meeting, there are four participants: two American women, Claire (45) and Linda (23), and two Japanese men, Tanaka (39) and Ikeda (37). Tanaka and Ikeda are the same officers who participated in the Japanese meeting. Unfortunately, because there are still few, if any, American-Japanese business meetings conducted in Japanese, cross-cultural data of this sort are more difficult to obtain. Thus, because the back-up data are cross-cultural meetings conducted in English, my examples and arguments tend toward illustrating uses and consequences of Japanese strategies extended to cross-cultural encounters.

Many native strategies appear to be used in cross-cultural interactions. For example, in the cross-cultural Personnel Meeting, the Japanese officer, Ito, spends a full eight minutes of the 28-minute meeting (almost 30 percent of the meeting time) on nontask-sounding talk; he discusses concerts and dinner parties, and asks the American officer, Sarah, what she has been doing recently. As I have thus far discussed, such a feature occurs in a business encounter because Japanese base their business relationships on personal ties, but Americans base theirs on a contract.

However, this difference alone creates problems in cross-cultural meetings; Americans criticize the perceived indecisiveness of the Japanese, and the Japanese criticize the alleged cold and ruthless behavior of the Americans. For example, in their videotape designed for American business negotiators in Japan, Tsukatani and O'Brien (1986) show how an American businessman is unable to close a deal after having spent long hours on it; the Japanese claiming that they simply had not reached a decision. In a moment of frustration, the American businessman questions the Japanese antagonists' inability to come to a decision: "Well, what have we been doing then?"

Likewise, the Japanese perceive the Americans as only interested in short-term profit, but not in establishing relationships over a long period of time. *Newsweek* (1990:22) reports: "The common image of American businessmen among Japanese is that they are 'totally interested in the bottom line, ruthless with people and overly interested in the short-term interests of shareholders.' " Moreover, in Japanese interaction, *honne* or frankness is often reserved for *uchi* (in-group) encounters; in cross-cultural *soto* (out-group) interaction, Japanese often present their *tatemae*, socially acceptable selves. Thus, they frequently cannot understand why Americans are so frank; they find such frankness misleading. This confusion then results in a Japanese misinterpretation of American behavior: the American directness is a disguise for *akushitsu na teguchi* (dirty tricks). Advising Japanese businessmen on how to negotiate with Americans, Graham and Sano (reported in Pfeiffer, 1988:152) warn: "Americans are generally honest and frank, the latter even to a fault. However, you should be aware that a few Americans may use dirty tricks."[3]

In conclusion, I have suggested that when conversationalists use their native strategies in cross-cultural business interactions, members of the opposing groups each feel as if the other group is intentionally using devious tactics to outsmart the other. To avoid such negative reactions, it is important that Americans and Japanese understand one another's communicative strategies and the different expectations about interaction in general, and about business in particular, which such strategies reflect: Americans expect within-group independence, but Japanese, nonconfrontation.

In the following chapter, and in Chapters 4 and 5, I present the comparative analyses of American and Japanese topic management. In these analytic chapters, I demonstrate that the American and Japanese bank officers use different topic-management strategies to reflect differences in underlying expectations for interaction. I begin each of these chapters with frequently heard negative evaluations of Japanese by Americans, and of Americans by Japanese to show the kinds of stereotypes that develop from misunderstood topic-management strategies and underlying interactional expecta-

---

[3] Americans have typically gone on-record more frequently with their negative evaluations of Japanese than vice versa. It is likely that this phenomena also occurs as a result of differences in American and Japanese expectations. Americans will state their opinions, even if they are sometimes negative because they feel that they are being honest (a postitive value for Americans discussed in this chapter). In contrast, Japanese emphasize nonconfrontation rather than the expression of thoughts through talk. Thus, Americans are more likely to state negative stereotypes more readily and explicitly than Japanese. In the confidence of *uchi* relations (among Japanese), Japanese do state negative sterotypes. However, these are often stated off-record in intimate relations.

tions. It is my hope that an awareness about differences in topic-management strategies and reflected interactional expectations serve the applied goal of abating the resentment so often caused by accumulated instances of American-Japanese cross-cultural miscommunication.

CHAPTER 3

DO-IT-YOURSELF VERSUS PRELUDES AND POSTLUDES: OPENING AND SHIFTING STRATEGIES IN TOPIC MARGINS

> Japanese are evasive and illogical, you never know what they're trying to say.

> Americans are blunt and insensitive, they just plow through with their own opinions, and spend little time cultivating relationships.

In Chapter 2, I described differences in American and Japanese interactional expectations; Americans and Japanese place antithetical emphases on the individual and the group, and on talk and silence. Furthermore, guided by the Cross-Talk model (Gumperz, Jupp, and Roberts, 1979) and the tradition of interactional sociolinguistics (Gumperz, 1982a; Tannen, 1984a), I argued that such differences in interactional expectations motivate the different strategies used by Americans and Japanese to manage topics. As the first of three analytic chapters, in this chapter, I focus on strategies used in topic margins; I examine the different ways in which the American and Japanese participants open and shift topics. Each strategy meets intracultural expectations for interaction: the American opening and shifting strategies satisfy their expectations of maintaining independence within the group; the Japanese strategies fulfills their expectation of nonconfrontation.

In the following, I present examples of the American and Japanese topic opening and shifting strategies in turn. In the American meeting, I illustrate that by referencing a predetermined agenda, a single officer opens his or her own topic, and names the "deal" for which s/he is responsible. The same officer-in-charge then closes his or her own topic with an explicit, verbal formula. In contrast, in the Japanese meeting, because a single officer is not in charge of a particular deal, the opportunity for topic opening is available to all officers. Furthermore, unlike the agenda that alerts the American officers to a general topic flow, the Japanese officers determine their topics locally; thus, it is critical that they show how each topic relates to others. The officers mark such relationships through the use of metacomments in topic openings. Finally, the officers do not conclude topics verbally, but instead, shift topics by allowing long pauses to develop between topics.

For each strategy, I show how participants organize their topics and meet their respective expectations for interaction. I also illustrate examples where native strategies of topic opening and shifting are used in cross-cultural communication encounters. Through such examples, I argue that because Americans and Japanese open and shift topics differently, they are likely to confuse and misunderstand one another in cross-cultural communication.

THE AMERICAN TOPIC-OPENING STRATEGY

Name Your Own Deal

In the American meeting, each participant, Craig, Karen, and Lynn, raises his or her own topics, by naming the "deals" for which s/he is responsible. There are seven major topics in the meeting: six deals plus an ad hoc "deal-listing" topic, which begins with a discussion on an absent meeting member's (Mark's) deals, and ends with the addition of any unmentioned deals which might warrant discussion. The seven major topics are listed in Table 3.1, with the names of the officers responsible for the deal, and the topic initiators.

Table 3.1 indicates that the officer responsible for the deal initiates his or her own topic. The exception is the last topic,

TABLE 3.1
OFFICERS-IN-CHARGE AND TOPIC INITIATORS IN THE AMERICAN MEETING

Topic	*Officer-In-Charge*	*Topic Initiators*
The Morrow Deal	Craig	Craig
The Courtney Deal	Craig	Craig
The Phelps Deal	Craig	Craig
The Brentnall Deal	Karen	Karen
The Garrison Deal	Karen	Karen
The Hinkley Deal	Lynn	Lynn
Deal Listing	Absent Officer/All	Karen

"Deal Listing," which is a topic to which all officers contribute. The officer, Karen, opens this topic, by introducing the absent member's (Mark's) topic: "I don't know what's happening with-, MC, or- CM, or whatever it is, on Mark's deal." Presumably, if Mark was present, he would have introduced his own deal.

For all other topics, the talk makes the "officers-in-charge" apparent; in talking about their deals, the participants use the first personal pronoun "I," and possessives such as "my" or "Mark's deal." Example 3.1 shows two excerpts with the referential cues, "I" and "my" indicating that the officer-in-charge opens his or her own topic.

Example 3.1

Topic	*Officer*	*Excerpt with Linguistic Cues*
The Courtney Deal	Craig	the other deal< uh that **I** have been spending most of my TIME on> , is Courtney<
The Hinkley Deal	Lynn	**my** deal- Hinkley-, it is a complicated deal<

In addition to such cues which indicate the officer responsible for the deal, I confirmed my judgment about the officer-in-charge in a follow-up discussion with a meeting participant, Karen. Thus, the American officers use specific linguistic cues to signal their "in-charge" status, and open their own topics. In this way, they meet their cultural and business expectation for individuality, as each officer-in-charge has the right to open his or her own topic.

As they open their own topics, the American officers explicitly name the deal; they consistently use the name of the deal and the word "deal" in all topic openings. Moreover, in five of the seven topic openings, participants use a linguistic structure of the form, NP = NP. The actual form used is one where the word "deal" and the name of the deal are placed on either side of the copula "is" to create the equation, "X is the deal," or "the deal is X." Because the two sides of the copula are reversable, these topic openings are much like quantities on either side of an equal sign (=) in a mathematical equation; thus, I refer to this American topic-opening strategy as a "verbal equation." Example 3.2a illustrates these verbal equations, and Example 3.2b shows the extracted equation constituents.

Example 3.2a

1.	Craig	all right first **deal** today **is Morrow**>
2.	Craig	the other **deal**< uh that I have been spending most of my TIME on> , **is Courtney**>
3.	Craig	uhm< . a:nd< the other **deal**< that I've started to work on **is Phelps**<
4.	Karen	**Brentnall**< **i:s**< ah **a deal** that is being- has MIXED reviews on the marketplace>
5.	Lynn	my deal- **Hinkley**-, it **is** a complicated **deal**

Example 3.2b

1.	(first)	deal	is	Morrow
2.	(the other)	deal	is	Courtney
3.	(the other)	deal	is	Phelps
4.		Brentnall	is	a deal
5.		Hinkley (it)	is	a (complicated) deal

The American officers thus frequently use a verbal equation, and always name their own deal to open topics. By naming the deal, each officer signals to other participants that s/he is the officer-in-charge; a particular deal is his or hers. Such "topic ownership" then gives the American officers their right to establish their individuality.

The Agenda

While each officer individually opens his or her own topic, all officers are afforded the occasion to do so. The "contract" that ensures that all officers have the opportunity to contribute relevant deals to the meeting is the agenda. Button and Casey (1988/89) inform us that when participants invoke a predetermined agenda in meetings, they acknowledge their mutual orientation to the known-in-advance status of topics and officers-in-charge. With such a shared context, the participants are then able to move smoothly through the business at hand as they ratify the right of the officer-in-charge to open his or her own topic. Thus, the agenda helps the American participants organize themselves complimentarily in the group, and express their support and respect for individual rights. In short, the agenda helps the American officers organize both the topics and themselves, and meet their expectation for within-group independence.

Linear Topic Organization

Several adjectives in the topic openings shown in Example 3.2b point to how participants organize their topics and coordinate their interaction. In three of the five verbal equations there are the adjectives, "first" and "the other" (Numbers 1-3 in Example 3.2b) which modify the word "deal," and precede the remaining core constituents of the verbal equation. While optional, these adjectives are significant because they show that Craig, the participant who opened these topics, had a specific order in mind. That is, by modifying the deals with these adjectives, Craig organizes his topics so that the "first deal" is constrained in the discourse to come before the "other deals."

Because Craig's topic organization suggested an underlying pattern, I examined the arrangement of topics in the American meeting in further detail. I found that there was an interactionally significant pattern: The American participants organized their topics so that a topic where the future outcome is best-known is talked about first; a topic where the future outcome is least-known is talked about later. Thus, in Example 3.2a, the topic on the Morrow deal is raised first because it is the deal nearest to completion. The second topic on the Courtney deal is a deal that is underway but is a newer transaction relative to the first Morrow deal. Finally, the third topic on the Phelps deal is a deal that has just begun, and is the newest transaction relative to the Morrow and Courtney deals. Craig therefore organizes his topics—the Morrow, Courtney, and Phelps deals—from the deal where the future outcome is best-known to the deal where the future outcome is least-known.

While verbal markers such as Craig's which explicitly mark a specific order in topic organization are not used in all topic openings, the pattern of ordering best-known to least-known deals is consistently carried out by all three participants throughout the entire meeting. For example, because Lynn's Hinkley deal is a "complicated" deal, the future outcome is uncertain, and thus, this deal is talked about toward the end of the meeting (in the second to last topic) rather than earlier. Furthermore, because the seventh topic involves a discussion of the absent meeting member, Mark, they are the deals least known about; hence, it is the last topic discussed.

The American pattern of ordering deals therefore reflects the participants' awareness of a predefined agenda—an agenda that necessitates the unidirectional ordering of topics. As Hall (1959:132) informs us:

> We keep constant track of all sorts of things which are otherwise identical and only distinguish between them because of their order. The seventh day is different from the first day, the middle of the week is different from the end, and so on.

Thus, since unidirectional ordering is a key feature in linear organization, the American topic organization may be seen as "linear." Such linearity helps fulfill the participants expectation for within-group independence because while topics are opened independently by each participant, by subscribing to the same linear organization of topics, participants are also able to interpret one another's organization in the group.

Positioning

I have thus far showed that the American officers open their own topics, and move through the topics by referencing a common agenda. In the actual encounter of the meeting, however, the officers must still position their topic openings with respect to the other meeting members; they must position themselves in the interaction. Substantiating Schiffrin's (1987) claim that discourse markers play a significant role in organizing conversational interaction, I find that the American officers often use discourse markers for interactional positioning. The officers used discourse markers in four of the seven topics, of which three also contain filled pauses. Discourse markers and the optional filled pauses typically occur in the fuzzy boundary of topics.[1] These "positioning markers" are shown in Example 3.3 below.

Example 3.3

1. **all right** first deal today is Morrow>
2. **uhm**< . **a:nd**< the other deal, that I've started to work on is Phelps<
3. **so**> o:n **uh:m**< . on Garrison< holdings, that's the deal we sold out of a couple of weeks ago>
4. **ok**< **uhm**< . **well uhm:**< . my deal- Hinkley-, it is a complicated deal>

By using positioning markers such as discourse markers and filled pauses, the American officers check their right to open topics, and negotiate their position for topic opening in the interaction. In short, positioning markers are a way of asking, "Can I open my topic?" Such positioning shows the American officers' respect for other individuals in the group; the participants can open their own topics, but they must make sure that their right to do so is ratified by other meeting members.

In sum, the American officers opened their topics by naming the deal, which frequently conformed to a verbal formula of the varieties, "X is the deal" or "the deal is X." They also followed the agenda that organized topics in a linear order from best-known outcomes to least-known ones. Finally, participants often used discourse markers with an optional filled pause to

[1] In a preliminary analysis, I included the following discourse markers in my corpus: a) and (then) (so), b) then, c) so (then), d) but, e) because, f) ok, g) all right, h) well, i) or (something). With the exception of (9) "or something" all discourse markers occurred in the utterance-initial position. Discourse markers do not include any of the above words when they were used in their traditional linguistic sense, that is, "and" as a conjuction, "but" as a disjunction, and so on. Also, I did not consider "ok" and "all right" discourse markers when they were used as a response or back-channel.

For filled pauses, I distinguished between the hesitation marker varieties, such as "uhh" and "uhm," and vowel-lengthened varieties. I found that there were more filled pauses of the hesitation marker variety in the American meeting than in the Japanese meeting, but more filled pauses of the vowel-lengthening variety in the Japanese meeting.

position their opportunity for topic opening. The American topic-opening strategy therefore reflects participant expectation of within-group independence, as officers express their individuality by presenting their own deals within the confines of the group.

THE JAPANESE TOPIC-OPENING STRATEGY

Anyone Can Open a Topic

In contrast, in the Japanese meeting, there is no officer-in-charge of a deal who opens his own topic; instead, any officer can open a topic. This absence of "topic ownership" is due to the following factors. First, in Japanese business practices, a single officer is not solely responsible for a business venture. Thus, unlike the American officers who have "deals" for which they are independently responsible, the Japanese officers are jointly responsible for their business transactions. In the encounter of the meeting, then, the Japanese officers do not have independent topics to report on and open. Japanese topic opening therefore reflects the Japanese style of group management and concensus decision making discussed in Chapter 2.

In Chapter 2, I also argued that the Japanese expectation for nonconfrontational interaction is based on the assumption that talk is untrustworthy. Thus, in contrast to Americans who use talk as a tool for decision making, Japanese participants work at drawing the focus away from talk, and toward the relationship of members in the group. Unlike their American counterparts, then, the Japanese participants are not keen on negotiating an opportunity to talk, or vying for a chance to open a topic. The Japanese strategy for topic opening therefore also reflects their view of talk.

Table 3.2 shows the topic openings in the Japanese meeting in which the participants—Tanaka, Ikeda, and Shimizu—discuss three topics. I identified the topics in the Japanese meeting in the same way as those in the American meeting. Because there is no agenda to distribute topics to each participant, the officer, Shimizu, does not open a topic, while another officer, Tanaka, opens two.

In the American meeting, each officer opened his or her own

TABLE 3.2
TOPICS IN THE JAPANESE MEETING

Topic	*Topic Initiator*
Work and Vacations	Ikeda
The Regional Meeting	Tanaka
The San Francisco Agency	Tanaka

topic as the agenda supported their right to do so. The agenda therefore guaranteed a minimum of one topic for each participant. In contrast, as shown in Table 3.2, a participant in the Japanese meeting, Shimizu, does not open a single topic despite the fact that there are equally as many topics as there are participants. This occurs because an agenda that distributes a topic to each participant is absent in the Japanese meeting. However, the absence of an agenda supports the Japanese expectation of nonconfrontational interaction, as it does not require everyone to begin using the negatively viewed talk by opening a topic.

Nakane (1970) notes that when interaction occurs between a superordinate and a subordinate member of a hierarchical frame, the conversation becomes the superordinate's one-sided sermon. However, the officers in the *uchi* (in-group) Japanese meeting are of the same rank; thus, as I discuss in further detail in Chapter 4, while Shimizu does not raise a topic, the amount of talk is distributed evenly among members in the meeting. In spite of this evenness in rank status and talk-distribution, if the issue of rank-difference is pushed, then Shimizu (40), the oldest member, has the relatively highest rank (as opposed to Tanaka (39) and Ikeda (37)). Shimizu, then, should be the one who opens topics most frequently and talks most on the topics. However, Table 3.2 shows that it is Tanaka who raises the most topics, and the youngest participant, Ikeda, who raises the first topic. Thus, although a greater age difference among participants may have different implications, in this *kachoo-kai* (Vice Presidents' Meeting), whatever difference there is in terms of age and rank seems to have little consequence.[2] Rather, because the participants have similar statuses in the company,

[2] All officers have the title, *kachoo*, or vice president. However, a Japanese businessman, Ishii (personal communication, 1990) has pointed out that titles are less meaningful in Japan than in the United States. From his perspective, he views American titles as somewhat "inflated."

they are *dooryoo* (colleagues) of more or less equal status. In such a group of equals, the opportunity to open topics is available to all; anyone can raise a topic. In this particular meeting, those "anyones" turn out to be Ikeda, once, and Tanaka, twice.

In sum, because Japanese view talk as untrustworthy, and topic opening initiates talk, it is not in the best interest of Japanese interactants to open topics, and hence introduce talk into their interaction. When the opportunity to open topics is available to everyone, this distributes the burden of talk to all, and no one is singled out to shoulder the responsibility of engaging in the negatively viewed talk. In short, the lack of topic ownership creates an ideal situation for Japanese to meet their expectation for nonconfrontational interaction, and only those who feel they can contribute nonconfrontationally will do so. Recalling S. Maynard's (1989:131) claim that Japanese participants do not have to "overtly" participate in narrative story building to remain an active member of a conversation, one does not have to open topics to be an active member in a Japanese meeting.

Metacommunicational Remarks, Eased Entry, and Talk-Distancing

In her study of Japanese conversation, S. Maynard (1989) shows how a subject in her study uses a "sentence adverbial" when introducing a new "theme" or topic. Her example is a subject's utterance: "*soo ie ba ne sono hanashi sugoi n da yo*" ("Speaking of that, there's a story that's really awful") (S. Maynard, 1989:62, including the translation), where the cue *soo ie ba* (speaking of that) is the sentence adverbial. S. Maynard illustrates how the subjects in her study used this strategy to begin a new theme.

In the following section, I show how the Japanese officers in my study also use adverbials to open their topics. These adverbials are couched in what S. Maynard (1989) calls "metacommunicational remarks"; metacomments about the interactional talk (*hanashi*) itself. Metacommunicational remarks occur in all topic openings in the Japanese meeting, and serve the Japanese expectation for nonconfrontation in the following ways. First, the Japanese officers use adverbials in their metacommunicational remarks to relate the upcoming topic with other topics.

Through adverbial cues that point to the relation of topics in the meeting, Japanese officers organize their topics by simultaneously signaling the merging but changing focus of topics.

Furthermore, the adverbials are contextualized in metacommunicational remarks which serve the purpose of "padding" topic openings, for a gradual and eased entry. This topic-opening strategy therefore contrasts with the up-front strategy of the Americans, as it averts surprises that might be brought about by abruptly introducing a new topic. Thus, metacommunicational remarks serve the Japanese expectation of nonconfrontational interaction as they smooth over the transitions between topics, and thereby create a less blunt interface between the participants themselves, as well as between topics.

Metacommunicational remarks also help the Japanese officers respond to their expectation of nonconfrontation as they draw the focus away from the negatively viewed talk. The officers achieve such talk-distancing by talking about their own talk from the point of view of a nonparticipant, third party. As they become an audience to their own talk, the officers draw the attention away from the conversation, and toward the sharedness of interaction.

Example 3.4 shows examples of metacommunicational remarks that occur in all topic openings in the Japanese meeting. Each metacommunicational remark comments on the conversation-to-follow, and contains the word, *hanashi*, which literally means "talk," and an adverbial which shows the way in which the current topic relates to others.

Example 3.4

1. **zenzen** **hanashi** ga chigaun desu kedo> kondo mata
   not-at-all **talk** (S) different is but next-time again

   beishuu kaigi arun desu yo ne< hachigatsu goro
   American-States meeting have is (E) (PF) August around

   ni>
   (TFN)

2. **dandan:**< shigoto no **hanashi** ni natte kimas- san
   gradually: work (P) **talk** (PU) become come San

   furanshisuko eijenshii o tsukuru nante **hanashi** wa
   Francisco Agency (D) make such a thing **talk** (T)

   zenzen tachigie nan deshoo ka ne:<
   not-at-all fizzle-out (wonder) is (presumptive) (Q) (PF)

TRANSLATION

1. This **talk** is **completely** different, but next time there is going to be an American regional meeting around August.
2. The **talk** is **gradually:** comin- towards work, I wonder if all that **talk** about making the San Francisco Agency has completely fizzled out.

By using the adverbials "*zenzen*" ("not-at-all") and "*dandan*" ("gradually") to comment on the relationship of topics with other topics, the metacomments in Example 3.4 help the Japanese officers manage the organization of topics, as well as their interaction.

Moreover, by talking about their own talk, the Japanese officers objectify it. This not only allows the officers to reaffirm their view of talk as "just talk," but it also grants the officers an opportunity to detach themselves from individualized talk ownership, and become an audience to their own interaction. By objectifying their talk, and shifting their point of view to that of a third, nonparticipant's, the Japanese officers do not feel as if they are partaking in the negatively viewed talk. M. Matsumoto (1988) reports that such distancing from the actual encounter also occurs in *Noh*, a classical form of Japanese dance. Using a concept called *riken-no-ken*, *Noh* artists remove themselves from the actual act of the dance, and see themselves through the eyes of the audience. In short, because metacommunicational remarks relate topics in the interaction and accomplish talk-distancing, they support Japanese topic management, as well as the expected achievement of nonconfrontational interaction.

Metacommunicational Remarks and Circular Topic Organization

The metacommunicational remarks in Japanese topic openings also reflect the circular organization of topics. That is, while the adverbials that comment on the *hanashi* (talk) are restricted to a particular conversational context, as a preface to topic openings, they are not constrained relative to the use of other adverbials. In other words, there is no prerequisite for the placement of one adverbial before another; "*zenzen*" ("not-at-all") can occur before "*dandan*" ("gradually"), and vice-versa. Japanese topic organization is therefore not characterized by the kind of linearity found in the American meeting; rather, like Hinds' (1983) and Odlin's (1989) description of Japanese writing, the Japanese officers organize their conversational topics circularly, as adjectives that indicate unidirectional ordering are replaced by adverbials which do not.

Instead of resulting in chaotic topic openings where participants open topics at random, the absence of linearity in Japanese topic organization helps the officers manage their topics and interaction. That is, circular topic organization promotes nonconfrontational interaction as it allows for a nonspecified ordering of topics; participants have the option to open topics in any order. This means that participants can hop back and forth among topics; returning to a previous topic that has already been determined as nonconfrontational, or dropping a topic that appears threatening (an aspect of topic shifting I discuss in further detail later in this chapter). In other words, by organizing topics circularly, the Japanese participants have the added benefit of reopening topics freely. While topic reopenings can occur in American interactions, they are marked. Japanese topic reopenings are unmarked because as shown in Example 3.4, metacommunicational remarks are used to introduce new topics as well as to reintroduce old ones. In short, circular topic organization as reflected in the metacomments show how topics can be brought up in any order, and how such flexibility supports the expected Japanese behavior of nonconfrontational interaction.

Metacommunicational Remarks in English

Earlier I introduced the notion that different strategies often result in negative evaluations in cross-cultural communication. Because writing is permanently recorded, it remains open for public scrutiny; thus, the criticism of non-native strategies in the genre of writing seems to be particularly high. American scholars frequently point to the absence of topic openings in books written in English by Japanese authors, and criticize their absence for obscuring readability.[3] For example, in a book review, Schooler (1989:867) notes that a Japanese-authored

[3] To my knowledge, there are no records of negative evaluations of Americans writing in Japanese. This probably results from the fact that there are fewer Americans who write in Japanese than vice versa.

book in English lacks "coherence," partly because "There is no introduction." Smitka (1989:850) makes a similar criticism: "The almost total lack of introductions makes it even harder to read." Smitka (1989:850) further goes on to say that instead of explicit topic openings, "in typical Japanese prose fashion, there are preludes." Thus, these critics suggest that Japanese often extend native writing strategies to English, and that these become obstacles for American readers; the extension of Japanese writing strategies to English is therefore evaluated negatively.

However, as I have shown, it is not that Japanese do not use "introductions,"—they do, but their introductions are different from the kinds that Americans might expect. As I illustrated previously, Japanese introductions are clearly indicated through the use of metacommunicational remarks, or what Smitka (1989:850) refers to as "preludes." The use of these metacomments makes topic organization clear to Japanese participants, but for Americans in cross-cultural communication, the nonnative strategy is confusing.

This is not an issue about whether or not mainstream English structures should be prescribed to nonnative speakers of English.[4] However, awareness of differences in conversational strategies and the reflected interactional expectations may lead to fewer negative evaluations and misunderstandings in cross-cultural communication. Thus, in topic openings, if we are aware of how metacommunicational remarks forewarn us about the changing focus of a topic, we can attend to that change, and follow the organization.

For example, in an article on silence in Japanese communication, the Japanese anthropologist, Takie Sugiyama Lebra (1987) shifts the topical focus from a discussion on the Japanese tendency to cultivate silence to an analogy about traditional music. She makes this transition by using the metacommunicational remark, "if I may digress a little" (Lebra, 1987:344). The metacomment clearly directs and prepares the reader toward the diversion, and topical coherence is not lost. Simi-

[4] This concerns the issue that as numerous nonnative "Englishes" emerge in systematically varying patterns, the rhetorical and conversational organization of "English" has become polysemic. Although I do not think that Japanese speak a recognized variety of English, my personal feeling is that non-traditional Englishes spoken by speakers as a first language (such as Indian English and Singaporean English) should be interpreted in their own right. For more on varieties of English, see, for example, Kachru (1982) and Smith (1983).

larly, in discussing aspects of Japanese communication, Doi (1982) clearly heads his paragraphs with the metacommunicational remarks: "Speaking of unanimous agreement" (p. 220), and "I am wondering if I have succeeded in making the Japanese patterns of communication intelligible to you" (p. 221).

The Japanese also use metacomments in oral interaction in English as well. In the recorded conversation of the Corporate Banking meeting (one of two cross-cultural meetings used for back-up data) a Japanese officer, Tanaka (the same officer who participates in the Japanese meeting), opens a topic with the metacommunicational remark, "before I forget this, uh:m, I just wanted-, want to let you know," and then goes on to tell the other officers about the results of a business transaction. With such a comment about the conversation-to-proceed, Tanaka's topic opening informs the other officers about where the topic is directed, thus organizing the topic-in-interaction. Thus, awareness of differences in topic openings can help us interpret, rather than misinterpret, the extended native strategies in cross-cultural communication.

In sum, I showed that a participant in the Japanese meeting does not open his own topic because a single officer is not solely responsible for a topic. Moreover, I demonstrated how topics are opened with a metacommunicational remark, which comments on the relation of the emerging topic with other topics. Finally, I argued that metacommunicational remarks help fulfill the Japanese expectation for nonconfrontation as the metacomment draws the focus away from the unfavorably viewed talk, and the circular organization allows participants the freedom to "hop around" topics.

TOPIC SHIFTS

D. Maynard (1980) and Shuy (1986), among others, have referred to the movement from one topic to another as "topic shifts"; Button and Casey (1984) call such discontinuous topic progression, "boundaried topic movement." Both the American and Japanese participants have strategies to shift topics; however, they use different strategies: The American participants use a verbal formula to close grouped topics in their own round, while Japanese participants do not close their topics, but use silence to shift topics instead.

The American Strategy

Shifts in the Nth Round Margin

In the American meeting, the officers close grouped topics in their own round. There are four such rounds; a round for each of the three participants, plus an additional round where an absent member's (Mark's) deals and other remaining deals are listed. The first round is Craig's, and contains three topics, the Morrow, Courtney, and Phelps deals; the second round, Karen's, with two topics—the Brentnall and Garrison deals; the third round, Lynn's, with one topic—the Hinkley deal. Thus, for Lynn, the topic and round margins coincide, but for Craig and Karen, who have more than one topic, there are several topic margins within their rounds. The final round belongs to everyone, as they all contribute additional deals that might warrant discussion. Table 3.3 presents the participants' rounds, their topics, and the participant who closes each round.

Table 3.3 shows that Craig closes his round with three topics, Karen closes hers with two, and Lynn closes hers with one. In addition, Lynn also closes the final, ad-hoc round which includes a number of deals, and begins with a discussion about the absent member's (Mark's) deal. If Mark had participated, however, it seems likely that he would have had a round of his own to close. In short, as Craig, Karen, and Lynn opened their own topics, they similarly close grouped topics in their own rounds. The American strategy for topic closing therefore again expresses each officer's individuality.

TABLE 3.3
ROUND CLOSERS IN THE AMERICAN MEETING

Round Number	*Topic*	*Officer-In-Charge*	*Round Closer*
1	The Morrow Deal	Craig	
1	The Courtney Deal	Craig	
1	The Phelps Deal	Craig	
			Craig
2	The Brentnall Deal	Karen	
2	The Garrison Deal	Karen	
			Karen
3	The Hinkley Deal	Lynn	
			Lynn
4	Deal Listing	Absent Officer/All	
			Lynn

The American officers further represent their individuality by uniformly using the formulaic expressions, "that's it" or "that's all" to explicitly verbalize the decisive closing of their own rounds. Example 3.5 shows these formulaic expressions.

Example 3.5

Round Number		
1	Craig	**that's all** I have>
2	Karen	anyway, I don't know, ah **that's all** I've got>
3	Lynn	anyway< **that's it** on the deal> and then< so I think **that's it** on the paper that we've got in the market>
4	Lynn	yeah< uhh so that- **that's it**- it's CLOSed on our books for right now<

As shown in Example 3.5, an explicitly verbalized expression which states, "that's all I have to say" follows each of the topics in the rounds of the American meeting. By using such verbalization at the end of their own rounds, the American officers not only inform each other that their part is complete, but also distinguish their own contributions to the meeting from others'. With such individualized conclusions, then, Craig, Karen, and Lynn each reassert their position as the officer-in-charge for the last time.

However, as the officers affirm their sense of individuality, they simultaneously cooperate with other group members. The predetermined agenda again aids in this process as it simultaneously distributes a round to each and every participant, and contains the expression of individuality within the confines of the group. By calling participant attention to a contract that distributes rounds equally, the officers invoke the agenda in the meeting to balance their concurrent need for individuality and community. Thus, as they focus on placing verbal formuli in the margin between their own round and others', each officer takes the opportunity to complete his or her own round, and lets others complete theirs. Such cooperation then helps the three officers meet their expectation for within-group independence.

The Final Shift: Definitively Finishing the Line

Collective interaction is further enhanced among the American officers as the meeting is jointly closed. The meeting closing follows the final round, where Lynn completes the ad hoc round with a verbal formula: "**that's it**- it's CLOSed on our books for right now." The excerpt of the joint meeting closing, or what Schegloff and Sacks (1982:73) refer to as a "terminal exchange," is shown in Example 3.6.

Example 3.6

Lynn	ok< [laughs] so< yup<
	[
Karen	**that's it**>
Lynn	yeah>
Karen	all right< , I think that uh **that's it** for< , do you have anything else< , ok> , all rightie<
	[
Craig	nope>
	bye<

As the terminal exchange in Example 3.6 shows, Karen uses the verbal formula "that's it" twice to close the meeting. Moreover, she *thinks* "that's it" for the meeting, but she makes sure that Craig and Lynn do not have any other items to discuss. Lynn and Craig then also chime in, assuring Karen that they are completely "done." Lynn shows her agreement following Karen's first verbal formula with "yeah," and Craig shows that he does not have anything further to contribute by responding to Karen's question, "do you have anything else?" with "nope."

In a follow-up conversation, I asked Karen how she and the other participants knew when to adjourn the meeting. She responded, "the meeting is adjourned when *everyone* feels satisfied that they have *talked* about everything there is to *talk* about until the next meeting," reflecting the definition of a conversational closing offered by Schegloff and Sacks (1982:73): "a point where one speaker's completion will not occasion another speaker's talk, and that will not be heard as some speaker's silence." Thus, as Karen ensures that all officers feel that they have "talked through" all the deals that required discussion, the meeting is brought to a close, and the officers complete the "line" of topics prescribed by the agenda. In short, as the American officers jointly close the meeting, they definitively and finally accomplish a linear organization of topics, and confer their last endorsement to the American expectation for within-group independence: "Let each and every individual say they're finished."

The Japanese Strategy

Shifts in the Nth Topic Margin

In contrast, in the Japanese meeting, there are no predetermined rounds or formulaic expressions that close topical talk; instead, topics are separated by long silences. In general, long silences (pauses greater than 1.5 seconds)[5] occur more frequently in the Japanese meeting than in the American: 103 instances of long pauses in the Japanese meeting as compared to only 20 cases in the American meeting. When long pause durations are totalled cumulatively for both meetings, long pauses in the Japanese meeting (107.45 seconds) amount to more than twice the duration of the long pauses in the American meeting (41.2 seconds). This translates to an average rate of 5.15 long pauses per minute in the Japanese meeting, and .74 long pauses in the American. Finally, an average pause in the Japanese meeting is longer than in the American; the longest pause in the Japanese meeting is 8.2 seconds, but the longest in the American is only 4.6 seconds.

More specifically, long pauses occur consistently between all topics in the Japanese meeting; however, in the American meeting, a long pause only occurs once between topics, and it occurs together with a verbal formula, "that's it." Furthermore, the average pause-time to shift topics in the Japanese meeting is 6.5 seconds, as compared to the average of 1.7 seconds to shift topics or 3.4 seconds to shift rounds in the American meeting. In short, the Japanese participants shift topics through long silences and take a longer time to complete the shift when compared to the American officers.

Example 3.7 shows an example of how the Japanese officers place such long pauses between topics to shift topics. In this exchange, an eight-second long silence occurs between the conclusion of a topic on work and vacation-taking in Japan, and the following topic on an upcoming regional meeting (the first topic opening illustrated in Example 3.4). The excerpt begins as

[5] In Chapter 4, I distinguish between short pauses, pauses under 1 second, substantial pauses, pauses between 1 and 1.5 seconds, and long pauses, pauses greater than 1.5 seconds.

Ikeda and Shimizu give some final comments on the notion that American firms allow for longer vacations than companies in Japan; in America, employees get two weeks off, but in Japan, they only get “a week at the most.”

Example 3.7

Ikeda	nihon da to saikoo issh- issuukan deshita kara> Japan is if at most one-week- one-week it was so
Shimizu	n> isshuukan desu yo> mhm a week it is (E)
→	{**8.20**}
Tanaka	zenzen **hanashi** ga chigaun desu kedo> kondo not-at-all **talk** (S) different is but next-time
	mata beishuu kaigi arun desu yo ne< again American-States meeting have is (E) (PF)
	hachigatsu goro ni> August around (TFN)

TRANSLATION

Ikeda	Because in Japan it was a week at the most.
Shimizu	Mhm, it's A WEEK.
→	{**8.20**}
Tanaka	This talk is completely different but, next time there is again going to be a regional meeting around August.

In this example, the shift in topics is identifiable through the explicit reference to that shift in the subsequent topic opening (shown in Example 3.4). That is where Tanaka says, “this talk is completely different but,” and then goes on to open the next topic on the regional meeting in August. Substantiating S. Maynard's (1989:59) finding that “pauses mark boundaries of thematic fields,”[6] in the Japanese meeting, long silences (more than 1.5 seconds) consistently signal topic shifts between the completion of a preceding topic and the initiation of a new topic.

Thus, despite the use of talk throughout the Japanese meeting, the series of topics are punctuated by silences. These

[6] However, later in her book, S. Maynard (1989:157) notes that lapses of 5 seconds or more are often filled by back-channels, fillers, laughter, and other uninterperatable sounds. Thus, the lapses are not completely void of noise.

silences are unlike the formulaic expressions that explicitly close topics in the American meeting, as they obscure the definitiveness of topic endings in the Japanese meeting. This implicit topic-shifting strategy has the important twofold function of not only drawing the attention of meeting members away from "what was being talked about," but also from "who was talking about it." Because talk is viewed unfavorably, obscuring talk is a necessary strategy in Japanese conversations. Further, attributing the negatively viewed talk to a single individual jeopardizes membership in the group. In other words, the Japanese topic-shifting strategy incorporates the simultaneous function of obscuring the topic under discussion, and the individuals talking about that topic. In short, the silence that replaces the verbal markings which point to "who said what up until now" refocuses participant attention from the individual talk to group interaction. Silence in topic-shifting is a way of saying, "we share the floor and the interaction, and we also share the burden of having to talk."

The Final Shift

Phase out of the meeting.

In the American meeting, the officers closed their meeting with a verbal formula of the variants, "that's it" or "that's all" as they did their own topics. Similarly, the Japanese officers shift from the ending of the last topic of "The San Francisco Agency" to the meeting closing by using the Japanese strategy for topic shifting: a long pause. Example 3.8 shows this shift, where two long pauses (with the durations of 2.5 and 4 seconds, respectively) follow the ending of the last topic, and precede the beginning of the meeting closing. As Kindaichi (1957) points out, because of the Japanese aversion to ending a conversation on a note of finality, these long pauses serve to gradually, "phase out" the meeting.

Example 3.8

Ikeda	nandaka chotto sorya muzukashii daroo somehow a-little that's difficult is (presumptive)
	ne:< d'tte: X ginkoo zentai no< , so- soshiki (PF) because X bank entire (P) organization
	kanri no shikata ga yappari< , soo yuu management (P) method (S) after-all that kind of

shuueki n- , ne< , shuueki de shibatteru wake
profit (PF) profit (U) tied reason

dakara>
so

Shimizu chotto muzukashii kamoshirenai ne:< sore wa>
a-little difficult might (FP) that (T)

{**2.50**}

Ikeda sono mondai no kaiketsu wa>
that problem (P) resolution (T)

Tanaka demo izure ni shite mo ne< , sono:<
but in-any-event uh:m

{**4.00**}

Ikeda jya< ma:< nanka toritome no nai hanashi deshita kedo<
well so: somehow incoherent talk it-was but

Shimizu soo desu ne<
that's true

Ikeda kyoo wa< osoku: narimashita kara kono hen de<
today (T) late it-has-become so here around (TFD)

Tanaka n< soo desu ne<
yeah that's right

TRANSLATION

Ikeda That's kind of difficult, because the entire management practices of Bank X [the officers' bank] is dependent on (tied to) that kind of profit.

Shimizu I guess it's a little difficult, that.

{**2.50**}

Ikeda The resolution of that problem.

Tanaka But in any event, uh:m

{**4.00**}

Ikeda Well, so:, the talk was kind of incoherent, but

Shimizu That's true.

Ikeda It's gotten late so, we'll stop about here today.

Tanaka Yeah, that's right.

Example 3.8 shows that the Japanese participants accomplish their final shift in the meeting by placing long pauses in the topic margin, and gradually and quietly phase out their conversation in the meeting. There is a notable difference, then, between the definitiveness in the end of the American meeting, and this one. As Harris and Morgan (1987:390) describe Japanese business conversations: "[Japanese] conversation transpires with ill-defined and shadowy context, never quite definite so as not to preclude personal communication." Furthermore, M. Matsumoto (1988) repeatedly reminds us that the *ma* (space) in Japanese conversation is impregnated with meaning; one of which is the silent rapport among conversationalists.

"Phasing out" talk is a technique that is frequently used in Japanese phone conversations. I have often laughed watching Japanese (including an introspective look at myself) end a telephone conversation, as they gradually move the receiver away from their ear, both parties fading away to each other. This is most likely a part of politeness phenomena, as no one wants to hear the sound of a crashing receiver or feel "hung up" on. When I once worked at a Japanese company, I recieved a manual called, "How to make a telephone call." In it is a section that reminds Japanese office employees of the proper way to dismiss oneself from a telephone conversation; phase out the conversation, and hang up the phone quietly.

Avoid confrontation: Drop the topic!

The last shift toward the meeting closing is further notable because it shows how the Japanese officers simply "drop" the increasingly confrontational topic of the "San Francisco Agency." As shown again for emphasis in Example 3.9, in this excerpt, a full-fledged confrontation seems imminent as the perspectives on instituting the San Francisco Agency as a supplemental financial arm to Bank X (in which the Japanese officers are employed) splits in two. Earlier in the topic, Tanaka, the initiator of the topic, presents the view that the institution of the San Francisco Agency would be both plausible and profitable, but the other two officers, Ikeda and Shimizu, disagree. The excerpt begins as Ikeda voices his disagreement and Shimizu follows. Following these expressions of disagreement, Tanaka appears to continue discussing the topic on the "San Francisco Agency": "*demo izure ni shite mo ne, sono:*" ("But in any event, uh:m"), but then simply aborts furthering his contribution to the topic. A 4-second pause follows, and Ikeda shifts topics to begin the meeting closing.

Example 3.9

Ikeda nandaka chotto sorya muzukashii daroo
somehow a-little that's difficult is (presumptive)

ne:< d'tte: X ginkoo zentai no< , so- soshiki
(PF) because X bank entire (P) organization

kanri no shikata ga yappari< , soo yuu
management (P) method (S) after-all that kind of

shuueki n- , ne< , shuueki de shibatteru wake
profit (PF) profit (U) tied reason

dakara>
so

Shimizu chotto muzukashii kamoshirenai ne:< sore wa>
a-little difficult might (FP) that (T)

{2.50}

Ikeda sono mondai no kaiketsu wa>
that problem (P) resolution (T)

Tanaka demo izure ni shite mo ne< , sono:<
but in-any-event uh:m

{4.00}

Ikeda jya< ma:< nanka toritome no nai hanashi deshita kedo<
well so: somehow incoherent talk it-was but

Shimizu soo desu ne<
that's true

TRANSLATION

Ikeda That's kind of difficult, because the entire management practices of Bank X [the officers' bank] is dependent on (tied to) that kind of profit.

Shimizu I guess it's a little difficult, that.

{2.50}

Ikeda The resolution of that problem.

Tanaka But in any event, uh:m

{4.00}

Ikeda Well, so:, the talk was kind of incoherent, but

Shimizu That's true.

Toward the end of topic of the San Francisco Agency, Ikeda and Shimizu note the problematic nature of its institution, and contend that, at best, it would be "difficult" ("*muzukashii*"). Ikeda sees the "difficulty" as occurring because: "*X ginkoo zentai no , so- soshiki kanri no shikata ga yappari , soo yuu shuueki n- , ne , shuueki de shibatteru wake dakara*" ("the entire management practices of Bank X [the officers' bank] is dependent on (tied to) that kind of profit). Similarly, in an earlier part of the topic, Shimizu also charges that it would be both unprofitable and against the management philosophy of Bank X to institute the San Francisco Agency, as he says to Tanaka: "*sore wa muri desu yo*" ("that's impossible"). As the topic becomes increasingly confrontational, it begins to jeopardize the stability of group unity. Tanaka, realizing the escalating contention in the topic, and his adversarial position in it, drops further discussion, and Ikeda shifts to the meeting closing. Thus, Example 3.9, shows how "topic-dropping" serves the Japanese expectation for nonconfrontation because it allows participants to shift out of potentially confrontational topics. Moreover, Tanaka abandons the topic inconspicuously, thus further supporting the Japanese expectation for nonconfrontation. That is, because the Japanese participants consistently shift topics in the same way, by pausing without verbal closure, a shift out of a confrontational topic is unmarked. Thus, when Tanaka drops the disputed topic and Ikeda shifts to the meeting closing, they jointly accomplish the shift unnoticeably. This contrasts with the American strategy which uses a verbal closing to shift topics; if the Americans dropped a confrontational topic, it is likely that it would call attention. In short, topic-dropping supports the Japanese expectation for nonconfrontation, as it grants participants the opporunity to discontinue confrontational topics inconspicuously.

Completing the loop.

Finally, the last shift toward the meeting closing is particularly illustrative as it shows how the beginning of the meeting closing corresponds to the Japanese topic openings described earlier. That is, as Tanaka drops the topic of the San Francisco Agency, a 4-second pause follows. Ikeda then takes the opportunity to move out of the intensifying confrontation and shifts topics. As Example 3.10 highlights, his beginning comment contains a metacommunicational remark which describes the foregoing "*hanashi*" (talk).

Example 3.10

Tanaka	demo izure ni shite mo ne< , sono:< but in-any-event uh:m
	{4.00}
Ikeda	jya< ma:< **nanka toritome no nai hanashi deshita kedo**< well so: **somehow incoherent talk it-was but**
Shimizu	soo desu ne< that's true
Ikeda	kyoo wa< osoku: narimashita kara kono hen de< today (T) late it-has-become so here around (TFD)
Tanaka	n< soo desu ne< yeah that's right

TRANSLATION

Tanaka	But in any event, uh:m
	{4.00}
Ikeda	Well, so:, **the talk was kind of incoherent**, but
Shimizu	That's true.
Ikeda	It's gotten late so, we'll stop about here today.
Tanaka	Yeah, that's right.

As Ikeda uses a metacommunicational remark to comment on the *hanashi* (talk), he uses the same strategy to begin the meeting closing as the participants did to open topics. Thus, it appears that Ikeda treats "the meeting closing" as if it were another topic. The Japanese officers then complete the "loop" in their circular organization of topics, as they end the meeting using the same strategy they used to begin it.

Furthermore, as Ikeda uses a metacommunicational remark to comment on the preceding *hanashi* (talk), he explicitly reasserts the Japanese view that talk is unimportant; he comments that the talk was "incoherent" ("*toritome no nai hanashi*"). Following Shimizu's agreement, "*soo desu ne*" ("that's true"), Ikeda then counters the negative remark about their talk with an empathetic, concluding statement which suggests his understanding that, "everyone must be tired after a long day": "*kyoo wa osoku: narimashita kara*" ("it's gotten late today, so"). With this remark, he stresses the prominent Japanese view that it is the maintenance of personal relationships in the group that is important, not the talk. Thus, as the American participants attain a sense of accomplishment by making decisions through talk, Japanese gain their satisfaction by reaffirming their personal ties.

In short, one way Japanese participants respond to their double bind of having to use the unfavorably viewed talk, is by using distributed silences following topics. By using this topic-shifting strategy, the Japanese can phase out of the meeting, drop a conversational topic, and come full circle in their organization of topics. The Japanese officers can then fulfill their interactional expectation of nonconfrontation.

Topic Margins and Cross-Cultural Communication

Philips (1985) argues that while there are some interactions that are structured through talk, others are structured through silence. The sum of 103 long pauses (longer than 1.5 seconds) in the Japanese meeting, but only 20 in the American meeting lends evidence to this claim: American interaction is structured through talk, but Japanese interaction is structured through silence. The substantially higher frequency of long pauses in the Japanese meeting than in the American meeting therefore suggests a considerably higher tolerance for silence by the Japanese, than by the Americans.

In addition to this generally higher tolerance for silences, the Japanese officers also allowed for longer lapses of silence in topic margins. In the Japanese meeting, the average pause time for topic shifting is 6.5 seconds, but in the American meeting, the average pause time to shift rounds is 3.4 seconds, and to shift topics is only 1.7 seconds. Thus, the American participants require less time to shift topics than the Japanese.

The greater amount of time necessary for Japanese to shift topics can create problems for both Americans and Japanese in cross-cultural communication. As the silence between topics expands, the Americans with a lower tolerance for silence may shift topics, and open a new one. This is likely to make the Japanese feel "crowded," as they are not given the opportunity to continue on the topic should they so desire. Scollon (1985) and Tannen (1984a) inform us that a lower tolerance for silence always leads to "interruption." Thus, the Japanese may feel "interrupted," and because the Americans seem as if they always get the "last word," the Japanese label Americans as "insensitive."

However, as talk accomplishes decision making for Americans, they verbally shift and open topics to work toward such decision making. To the Americans then, the Japanese strategy for topic shifting seems to leave a topic "hanging"; topics appear to have been "dropped" rather than completed. Topic organization is then seen as "illogical," and the Japanese seem "evasive." Pointing to how the lack of summaries inhibits readability, Schooler (1989:867) and Smitka (1989:850) criticize the lack of conclusions in books written in English by Japanese authors, as they did their lack of introductions. Instead of definitive conclusions, as Smitka (1989:850) argues, there are numerous "postludes."

As I argue in the following section, these "postludes" are actually new topics introduced following long pauses. As I have thus far discussed, the Japanese strategy for topic shifting differs from the American because it does not close off topics verbally, but separates them with emerging silences. Example 3.11 shows how a Japanese officer, Ito, uses such silences to shift topics in the Personnel Meeting (another cross-cultural meeting used as back-up data). However, because he does not verbally close previous topics, and continuously adds new topics, his topic management is likely to confuse cross-cultural interactants.

Example 3.11

1. and uhh< **last one**, is s- quite personal> the uhh, you know Kenny> , of the international> bank> HE just gave me> uhh his daughter's, uhh, uh resume>

2. I think the< **last one**< , maybe you have received the letter< , through me< uhh . s- uhh Santa Clara Valley>

3. and also **one thing**< **anoth- another personal thing**< my< uhh daughter-in-law> my o- oldest son's wife> she got- she got- n- she got a job>

4. **one more thing**< [talking to himself, very low volume] Richard to uh um uhh, uhh< what's that u oh< I forgot> oh> , how 'bout the Sai- Sai Takeda's the uh<

In Example 3.11, Ito opens two of his topics by saying the item for the business-at-hand is the "last one." However, he then subsequently adds three more, using the metacommunicational remarks, "last one," "one thing, anoth- another personal thing" and "one more thing." All these topic openings follow a pause of over 1.5 seconds; thus, Ito extends a Japanese strategy for managing topic margins (shifting and opening) to the cross-cultural meeting.[7]

I observed a comparable extension of strategies in an academic meeting, where a Japanese speaker used "In conclusion" twice. As it turned out, both conclusions were actually the beginnings of new topics; each time the speaker addressed different aspects of Japanese reactions to U.S. foreign policy. The key observation here is that the so-called conclusions *followed*pauses. Although I was not able to measure the length of these pauses, it appears that in the cross-cultural session where he delivered his paper in English, the Japanese speaker also used a native strategy to manage topic margins.

The use of such a native strategy in cross-cultural interaction produces a quality of a never-ending topic for Americans; the organization of topics seems "incoherent" (Schooler, 1989), and full of "postludes and preludes" (Smitka, 1989). However, as I have argued, the Japanese strategy is both shared and meaningful in intracultural interaction. In communicating across cultures, then, interactants must be aware of differences in strategies for topic management; the different ways in which various groups shift and open topics in margins. Thus, as I have illustrated in the particular examples above, cross-cultural participants who interact with the Japanese must not only be able to "distinguish between rhetorical pauses and turn relinquishing pauses" as Gumperz (1982a:160) points out, but also between these and pauses which create the possibility for shifting topics in the emergent and expanding silence between topics.

CONCLUSION

In summary, I compared the different ways in which the American and Japanese officers opened and shifted topics in

[7] It is interesting to note that in this cross-cultural Personnel Meeting, Ito spends the first 8 minutes on nontask sounding talk. Here, he talks about going to concerts and places he has been dining. He also asks Sarah about the kinds of things she has done.

business meetings. The American officers opened topics by naming the deals for which they were responsible, and closed their own rounds with a verbal formula. This emphasis on individuality was then balanced by the agenda, a contract which assured the distribution of topics to all participants. In contrast, any Japanese officer could open topics, which were padded with a metacommunicational remark. To shift topics, the Japanese participants contextualized long pauses in between topics.

I attributed these differences in topic management to a more profound difference in cultural expectations. The American officers achieved their expectation for within-group independence as each officer individually opened and closed his or her own topic, but as prescribed by the agenda, used the same linear organization of topics, and restricted their talk on topics to within the confines of the group. The Japanese officers fulfilled their expectation for nonconfrontation through circular topic organization and talk distancing, as they diverted their attention from the inherently confrontational nature of talk, as well as from specific instances of particularly controversial talk. Such purposeful talk distancing then helped the Japanese refocus their attention toward the relatedness of the group.

De Mente (1989), March (1988), Thian (1988), Tung (1984), Van Zandt (1970) among other researchers of American-Japanese cross-cultural business negotiations cite numerous examples of how differences in interactional behavior often lead to frustration among cross-cultural business interactants. In interactional sociolinguistics, Gumperz (1982a) and Tannen (1984a) have made the point that increased contact does not automatically result in cross-cultural understanding. Instead, as I have argued, accumulated interactions between Americans and Japanese have resulted in situations where both feel that the other group is behaving in inappropriate ways. Thus, differences in topic management often lead to the reinforcement of stereotypes: "Americans are blunt and insensitive"; "Japanese are illogical and evasive." Misunderstanding the different strategies used in topic margins is, then, one way in which such stereotypes are kept alive.

CHAPTER 4

TALK IN TOPICS: LINES OF LOGIC AND CIRCLES OF RELATIONSHIPS CONTINUED

> Japanese beat around the bush, they make lots of irrelevant and anecdotal points.
>
> Americans are loud and aggressive, they just steamroll over us with their own views.

In cross-cultural communication, Americans and Japanese continually misunderstand one another as each group judges the other according to their own expectations for interaction. In Chapter 3, I compared strategies in topic margins and showed that the American participants fulfilled their expectation of within-group independence as they opened and closed their own topics through explicit verbalization. On the other hand, the Japanese officers accomplished their expectation of nonconfrontation as they deemphasized what they regard as potentially harmful talk, and stressed agreeable contact instead.

In this chapter, I examine the talk in topics, or what Keenan and Schieffelin (1975) call "discourse topic." I compare the ways in which the American and Japanese officers distribute their talk in topics, and how they make topical points. Ethnomethodologists (reported in Atkinson and Heritage, 1984) describe such continuous movement through topics as "stepwise" movement, and scholars such as Danes (1974), Givon

(1983), S. Maynard (1989) and Shuy (1986) have devised formal models to characterize continuous topical or thematic progression.

For both the American and Japaese groups, I find a corresponding pattern between the strategies they use to manage topical talk and those they used to manage margins. In the American meeting, the officers-in-charge follow their own topic openings with relatively independent talk contributions to their own deals. Furthermore, the officers organize their talk by arranging topical points in a linear order: earlier points state the present status of the deal, middle ones, the background, and final points, the future expectations of the deal. In contrast, in the Japanese meeting, topical talk is distributed relatively evenly among all officers. Moreover, circularity characterizes the organization of the Japanese talk as the officers make points by giving examples.

Each of the strategies for topical talk enhances the American and Japanese expectations for interaction. The American participants achieve within-group independence as each and every officer delivers his or her own deal according to a uniformly linear organization. The Japanese officers accomplish nonconfrontation as the officers arrange their points in a circular organization, and collectively redistribute the focus of the group from topical content to interactional contact. In the following section, I compare first talk distribution, then point making, to show how the American and Japanese participants manage these aspects of topical talk to fulfill their respective expectations for interaction.

TALK DISTRIBUTION: AUTONOMY VERSUS INTERDEPENDENCE

In her study comparing Indians of the Warm Springs Reservation to Anglos, Phillips (1976) finds that talk is distributed more evenly among the Indians than among the Anglos. I find a parallel difference between the Japanese and the Americans in my study; the Japanese distribute their topical talk more evenly than the Americans. The continuum of autonomy to interdependence can be shown in several different ways by measuring the amount of talk through tone-units and turns. Thus, I first compare the distribution of tone-units in topics, and then I examine differences in strategies for turn distribution. I begin each of the talk-distribution analyses with an explanation about how I measured these units.

Tone-Unit Distribution

Definition

I used tone-units to quantify the amount of speech in the American and Japanese meetings because they provided a more meaningful measurement for comparative purposes than word-count tabulation, the most prevalent method of measuring the amount of conversational speech. My conclusion is based on a small-scale experiment that asked a group of 10 native Japanese speakers to intuitively parse out the words in the following Japanese sequence: "*ossharanakattatteosshattemasendeshitakke*" (polite form of "weren't you saying that s/he didn't say that?"). The results showed 10 different parses, ranging from 0 to 9 boundaries for "words." Thus, because Japanese is an agglutinative language and actual word boundaries do not exist as in English, I used a pause-bounded tone-unit as the common denominator across the American and Japanese meetings.

Labels for the tone-unit in English discourse include: "idea unit," "information unit," "tone group," "breath group," and "phonemic clause" (reported in Brown and Levinson 1987:155). Labels for a slightly smaller unit in Japanese discourse include Clancy's (1982) "intonation group" and S. Maynard's (1989) "pause-bounded phrasal unit." For this study, my definition of a tone-unit draws most directly from Chafe's (1979, 1980, 1985) work on "idea units" or "information units," Halliday's (1967, 1978) description of "tone groups" and S. Maynard's (1989) definition of "pause-bounded phrasal units." All three scholars argue for a degree of sociopsychological reality in the realization of a tone-unit, and Chafe and S. Maynard describe its pause-bounded characteristic. However, to account for the smaller segments of speech in Japanese, S. Maynard's (1989) definition of the pause-bounded phrasal unit differs from Chafe's (1979, 1980, 1985) and Halliday's (1967, 1978) as her unit is a phrase, while theirs is a clause. S. Maynard's (1989:24) definition of the "PPU" (pause-bounded phrasal unit) is "lexical items plus function words such as particles" set apart by pauses. Clancy (1982) also argues that Japanese "intonation groups" are shorter than clauses.

My definition, then, is based on the assumption that speakers group their talk into communicative chunks of pause-bounded speech. As these pauses range in length, I classified them into three groups: a) a short pause, less than 1 second in duration; b) a substantial pause, between 1 and 1.5 seconds; c) a long pause, more than 1.5 seconds. Brown and Yule (1983:163) also group pause lengths in three categories. However, the names and the lengths of each category vary somewhat from mine.

I found that although there is a notably greater frequency of long pauses in the Japanese meeting than in the American (5.15 per minute in the Japanese meeting as opposed to 0.74 in the American), the incidence of total pause occurrence (all categories) is equivalent by the minute: An average of 14 pauses occur in both meetings. In other words, the duration of each pause differs, but the frequency of pausing does not. Thus, because the data show a comparable distribution of pauses in the two meetings, I counted each pause-bounded chunk of speech as a single tone-unit. Moreover, as Halliday (1967, 1978) points out, tone-units also typically contain an intonational contour and a tonic syllable. Ultimately, I view tone-units as structured through a rhythmic rather than phonological or syntactic organization.

Initially, I included back-channels in my tabulation to arrive at a "gross sum" of tone-units. After I counted the number of back-channels (which I discuss in Chapter 5), I then subtracted them from the "gross sum" of tone-units to produce a "net sum." Finally, I averaged both the net sum of tone-units as tone-units-per-minute, to standardize the time differential produced by different meeting lengths.

Analysis

An analysis of the proportional distribution of tone-units in topics demonstrates that the American officers talk most about their own deals which they themselves opened, but that this is not necessarily true for the Japanese. Table 4.1 shows the proportional distribution of tone-units in each topic in the American and Japanese meetings. The figures for each officer are a percentage of the net sum of tone-units for each topic, and hereafter, an asterisk (*) indicates a topic-initiator.

Table 4.1 shows that relative to other participants in the

TABLE 4.1
PROPORTIONAL DISTRIBUTION OF TONE-UNITS PER TOPIC

Meeting	Topic	Proportional Distribution of Tone-Units		
American				
		Craig	*Karen*	*Lynn*
	1 Morrow	*85.33	13.33	01.34
	2 Courtney	*82.52	16.30	02.18
	3 Phelps	*79.49	15.38	05.13
	4 Brentnall	00.48	*87.20	12.32
	5 Garrison	05.93	*87.29	06.78
	6 Hinkley	05.56	44.44	*50.00
	7 Deal-Listing	18.02	*50.45	35.53
Japanese				
		Tanaka	*Ikeda*	*Shimizu*
	1 Work & Vacations	43.73	*30.55	25.72
	2 Regional Meetings	*42.55	48.40	09.05
	3 S.F. Agency	*47.71	22.94	29.35

American meeting, each officer talks the most about his or her own deal. That is, each officer takes more than 50 percent of the tone-units in his or her own topic: Craig takes an average of over 82 percent of the tone-units in talking about his deals, "Morrow," "Courtney," and "Phelps"; Karen, over 87 percent in talking about her topics, the "Phelps" and "Garrison" deals; Lynn, 50 percent, in talking about her topic the "Hinkley" deal. Conversely, with the exception of the last, ad hoc topic which belongs to all participants, there is an officer whose talk occupies less than 6 percent of the proportional distribution of talk across participants. Thus, each of the officers carries his or her own topic(s) through fairly autonomously, as other officers restrict their participation to the role of listenership.

Moreover, because the topics in which Craig, Karen, and Lynn talk the most or take the greatest number of tone-units are the topics that they initiated, the American officers talk most on the topics they themselves opened. This even holds for the last topic of "Deal Listing," which Karen opened, and where she talks for more than 50 percent of the talk in that topic. Thus, for all topics in the American meeting, the officers talk more on the topics they initiate. In conjunction with the findings of Chapter 3, then, the American officers open, deliver, and close their own topics autonomously.

In contrast, Table 4.1 shows that the Japanese officers do not necessarily talk most on topics they open. That is, although

Tanaka talks most on the topic of the "San Francisco Agency" which he initiated, Ikeda talks more on the topic of the "Regional Meeting" which Tanaka also initiated. In addition, Ikeda opened the topic on "Work and Vacations," but Tanaka takes a greater number of tone-units in that topic. Thus, for two of the three topics discussed in the Japanese meeting, a participant who did not open the topic talks more.

This contrast lends further evidence to the fact that for the Americans, topic initiation means topic ownership, but that for the Japanese, it does not. Each American officer presumably talks most on his or her own topic because s/he is most informed about that topic; s/he is the officer-in-charge. On the other hand, because there are no officers-in-charge in the Japanese meeting, topics are shared among the Japanese officers, and an officer's topic initiation does not necessarily result in his singular contribution to that topic. Talk distribution strategies therefore also reflect differences in American and Japanese syles of business.

Furthermore, unlike the uneven distribution of talk-time in the American meeting, the talk in the Japanese meeting is fairly evenly distributed among officers. The exception is the second topic of the "Regional Meeting." This topic, however, occupies the shortest amount of time in the meeting (13 percent of the total meeting time). Moreover, all officers in the American meeting take 50 percent or more of the tone-units in a single topic; all officers in the Japanese meeting take 49 percent or less. In an average topic, then, the difference between the most and least talkative participants in the American meeting is about 75 percent (78.64.3.44), but only about 27 percent (46.61-19.24) in the Japanese meeting. Thus, as compared to the American officers, the Japanese distribute their talk among officers fairly evenly; topical talk in the Japanese meeting is relatively interdependent. As I pointed out earlier, such evenness in talk distribution is not likely to occur when the rank statuses among participants are not equal (see Nakane, 1970). In this *kachoo-kai* (Vice Presidents' Meeting), however, the officers' ranks are comparable; hence, the evenness in talk distribution.

The American bank officers further emphasize their in-charge status as they spend the majority of their individual talk-time discussing their own deals—the topics they initiated. Once again, this is not necessarily true for the Japanese participants; the Japanese do not always expend more of their own talk on a topic they initiated. Table 4.2 shows the proportion of each participant's personal talk-time spent on topics initiated (tone-units of each participant in a particular topic divided by the total tone-units of each participant). In the American meeting, the percentages for Craig and Karen are collapsed to reflect the percentages of individual talk-time expended on topics in their own rounds.

Table 4.2 therefore shows that the American officers spend most of their individual talk-time on their own deals, and on topics that they initiated. The Japanese, on the other hand, do not necessarily spend most of their own talk-time on the topics they initiated. The exception here is Ikeda's talk-time as he expends the largest amount of his talk in discussing the first topic of "Work and Vacations" which he raised. However, all participants spend most of their talk in discussing this topic, as it is the longest topic in the meeting (70 percent of the total meeting time).

In addition, in comparison to the American officers, the Japanese distribute their own talk-time relatively evenly across topics. On average, the difference between the highest and lowest talk-participations for each topic is about 60 percent (66.65%—6.67%) for the American officers, but only about 18 percent for the Japanese (42.52%-24.13%). Thus, the Japanese officers distribute their talk-time fairly evenly across topics, as well as among participants; the Americans contribute most of their individual talk-time, and take the greatest proportion of topical talk in their own topics.

Fundamentally, these different talk-distribution strategies

TABLE 4.2
PERCENTAGE OF INDIVIDUAL TALK-TIME SPENT ON TOPICS

Meeting	Topic	Proportional Distribution of Tone-Units		
American				
		Craig	*Karen*	*Lynn*
	Morrow/Courtney/ Phelps	*84.45	08.19	04.46
	Brentnall/Garrison	03.36	*63.50	43.54
	Hinkley	12.19	28.31	*52.00
Japanese				
		Tanaka	*Ikeda*	*Shimizu*
	Work & Vacations	42.50	*40.25	49.69
	Regional Meetings	*25.00	38.56	11.00
	S.F. Agency	*32.50	21.19	39.31

reflect differences in respective expectations for interaction. As the American officers deliver their own topics, they reassert their individual autonomy, and their "right to be heard" (Edelsky, 1981:401). Further, the agenda predistributes the talk-time to all participants, and as supporting participants respect the right of the officers-in-charge to present their own deals, they promote group-internal understanding. Similarly, as Japanese officers distribute roughly equal amounts of talk to each other and to each topic, no one participant appears to say more or know more about a topic. Such "sameness" satisfies the Japanese expectation of nonconfrontation as individual boundaries are blurred in favor of collective and symmetric interaction.

Turn Distribution

Definition

Following Sacks, Schegloff, and Jefferson (1974) in ethnomethodology, and Duncan and Fiske (1977) in social psychology, "turn-taking" or "turn exchange" has been studied extensively in conversation. For example, in English, Denny (1985), Duncan and Fiske (1977, 1985) and Sacks, Schegloff, and Jefferson (1974) have developed models for turn-taking; S. Maynard (1989) has studied turn-taking and "turn-yielding signals" in Japanese conversation; Edelsky (1981), Erickson (1982a), Fiksdal (1986), Gallois and Markel (1975), Gumperz (1982a), Hayashi, (1988), Philips (1976), Shultz, Florio, and Erickson (1982), and Tannen (1981a, 1982a, 1983, 1984a) have studied turn-taking from various comparative vantage points.

An alternative concept to the "turn" is the "floor." Edelsky (1981:401) defines the "floor" as having: a) one or more turns, b) a space (that part of a chamber occupied by members), c) participants (members of an assembly), and d) a right to be heard. Erickson's (1982a:47) definition of the "floor" is: " a sustained focus of cognitive, verbal, and nonverbal attention and response between speaker and audience." A number of studies have examined cultural influences on "floor" management. For example, see Edelsky (1981) for a comparison of sex differences; Hayashi (1988) for a comparison of American and Japanese conversation; Erickson (1982a) and Shultz, Florio, and Erickson (1982) for a study of cultural influences on Italian-American conversations. Although the approaches and techniques for turn analysis differ among researchers, they similarly conclude that turns distribute talk among participants, and that they systematically regulate and organize conversational interaction.

In my study, I counted a new turn if it was: a) preceded by another participant's turn, and/or b) preceded by a long pause (longer than 1.5 seconds). I counted a turn following a long pause as a new turn because as S. Maynard (1989) and Tannen (1985c) point out, pauses belong to all conversational participants. Thus, any participant has the opportunity to take a turn following a long pause. Furthermore, if overlapping speech or "sync talk" (Hayashi, 1988) occurred, I counted each participant's speech as separate turns. (See Tannen, 1984a, for how overlap creates rapport in conversations among Jewish Americans, and Hayashi, 1988, for how "sync talk" creates a supportive environment for Japanese conversation.) I did not count back-channels as new turns unless non-back-channelling utterances immediately followed them.

Analysis

In an analysis of turn distribution in the American and Japanese meetings, I find that each of the strategies correspond to the pattern of talk distribution illustrated earlier in the comparative analysis of tone-unit distributions. Table 4.3 shows that for five of the seven topics in the American meeting, an officer who initiates a topic takes the greatest number of turns in it. In contrast, for only one of the three topics initiated in the Japanese meeting does an officer who initiated the topic take the highest number of turns.

Thus, replicating the pattern of talk distribution found in the analysis of tone-units, most of the topics in the American meeting have a participant who takes more than 50 percent of the turns in the topic s/he initiated. In the Japanese meeting, Tanaka takes 50 percent of the total number of turns in only one topic, the "Regional Meeting," but again, this topic occupies a relatively short period of the meeting time.

The exceptions in the American meeting are the last two topics of "Hinkley" and "Deal Listing." The topic of "Deal Listing" is fairly evenly distributed among the American officers because all American officers contribute to this ad-hoc topic. The topic of the "Hinkley" deal warrants further discussion. In this topic, although Lynn talks more than Karen (Table 4.2 showed that Lynn takes 50% of the tone-units in the topic,

TABLE 4.3
PROPORTIONAL DISTRIBUTION OF TURNS PER TOPIC

Meeting	Topic		Proportional Distribution of Tone-Units		
American					
			Craig	*Karen*	*Lynn*
	1	Morrow	*60.00	20.00	20.00
	2	Courtney	*50.00	40.00	10.00
	3	Phelps	*53.33	20.00	26.67
	4	Brentnall	00.01	*59.46	40.53
	5	Garrison	04.76	*61.91	33.33
	6	Hinkley	17.65	61.76	*20.59
	7	Deal-Listing	22.45	*36.73	40.82
Japanese					
			Tanaka	*Ikeda*	*Shimizu*
	1	Work & Vacations	40.00	*38.10	21.90
	2	Regional Meetings	*50.00	08.33	41.67
	3	S.F. Agency	*40.00	15.00	45.00

but Karen only took 44.44%), Karen takes a greater number of turns (61.91%) than does Lynn (20.59) most likely for the following reasons. First, the "Hinkley" deal is a relativley new transaction, which Lynn describes as "complicated." In the first part of the topic, Lynn tells the other meeting participants what she knows about the status of the deal (a subject I discuss in further detail in the following section on point making). However, because little is known about the outcome of the deal, the officers hypothesize about its future possibilities. In the middle of such conjectures, Karen takes several turns to tell Lynn about a potential client who might be interested in the "Hinkley" deal. Example 4.1 shows the beginning part of this exchange, where Karen introduces the idea of selling a portion of Lynn's deal to a certain "regional bank."

Example 4.1

Karen oh- we've got one bank that has- one of Cheryl's<- where is Cheryl today<

Lynn she's at a breakfast>
[
Craig a breakfast>

Karen oh that's right> yeah uh:m< , she< has one regional bank that< has< indicated that they are very close to having a twenty five million assignment>

Lynn	m:< yeah so-
	[
Karen	or a twenty five million approval and they wanted an assignment> , and uh:m< , ah at our pricing>

This deal is problematic, as Lynn describes the Hinkley deal as one with "many hidden aspects to the deal," and therefore likely to be "slow in selling." As a slow sale is unprofitable for the bank, Karen offers a suggestion of a potential buyer. Moreover, another indicator of the problematic nature of the Hinkley deal is that although the officers had been using acronyms to preserve the anonymity of competitors and buyers, on several occasions in this topic, Lynn and Karen give the actual name of competitors and potential buyers. This then suggests that many of the "hidden aspects" were unfamiliar to the other officers, so that names of interested parties had to be clearly spelled out. Thus, the great proportion of unknown factors about the Hinkley deal, and Karen's attempt to resolve its problematicity may account in part for the greater number of turns that she takes in Lynn's topic.

Another plausible reason why this counterexample occurred may be because Lynn takes long, monologic turns in this topic. That is, earlier I showed that Lynn *talked* more than Karen (indicated in the figures in Table 4.2) on the topic of the "Hinkley" deal. However, because she takes fewer turns than Karen, Lynn talks more in each turn. For example, Example 4.2 shows how Lynn takes a long turn to explain how their position in the market is stronger than another lender's (dubbed "BT").

Example 4.2

Lynn	I know that they're- I KNOW that WE are better than BT< , and I know that people are expressing reLUCtance to BUY from them< because- they're n- they're not known to hold any portion of the deal< and< , I- spoke to one, company< uh just the other day< 'n' 'he said oh great> I'm glad you're offering it> because I don't want to buy from them> even though if they're- , they're meeting up> people have- some people have- GONE to that meeting< uhm< I don't , I haven't talked to anyone< directly> who's been I've talk to other people who've been< inVIted< , and never were sent a package>
Karen	oh really<

Lynn takes such monologic turns frequently in her topic of the "Hinkley" deal. That is, in an average turn in this topic, Lynn speaks for about 11.57 tone-units, but Karen only speaks for about 3.43 tone-units. Thus, although Lynn's proportional distribution of turns is less than Karen's, she still talks more than Karen on her own deal.

Furthermore, the American officers take long, monologic turns even in short and uncomplicated topics. As I described in Chapter 3, the deal where the future outcome is most known is talked about first. Thus, unlike the "complicated, Hinkley deal," the earlier deals occur first because they are less problematic, and hence, resolved in a shorter period of time. For example, the shortest topic is Craig's topic of the "Morrow" deal. Following his opening "all right first deal today is Morrow," Craig begins a long, monologic report on his own deal. Example 4.3 shows Craig's long turn in the beginning of his topic, punctuated only once by Lynn's back-channel "o:h," and ended with Karen's question about the deal.

Example 4.3

Craig   all right first deal today is Morrow> , a:nd we are in< , ah final documentation< we have brought in< this- ah we have seven assignments< a:nd we brought in five banks< , LAST friday> ah we had a- interesting- feature there because< , eighty eight percent of the loans were rolling over on that one day>

                [

Lynn   o:h

                   [

Craig   ah so there was a big emphasis to<- , bring the banks in on the FIFTH< to avoid a break funding cost> , we have two additional banks to bring in< , and hopefully we'll be able to do that< , in the next week or so> uh:< I'm gonna be out next week< so this is s- to some extent gotta be arranged AROUND< , uh the days that I'll be GONE> , BUT> , um if you DO have any reQUESTS> u:m if you HEAR of any banks that are looking for that- paper< um I have one seller< who has now come back to ME< and asked if we would essentially do a brokerage deal for him>

Karen   is that the same one that we had last week<

An analysis of turn size shows that such monologic turns occur frequently in the American meeting, particularly when compared to the length of turns in the Japanese meeting. That is, in the American meeting, the average number of turns exchanged in a topic is 24.43 (171 turns/7 topics), but in the Japanese meeting, an average topic contains as many as 50.67 turns. This difference in average turn size shows that the Japanese officers generally exchange turns more rapidly than their American counterparts. Example 4.4 shows an example of such rapid turn exchanges which follow Tanaka's opening of the shortest topic, the "Regional Meeting."

Example 4.4

<table>
<tr><td>Tanaka</td><td>zenzen hanashi ga chigaundesu kedo> kondo
not-at-all talk (S) different is but next-time

mata beishuu kaigi arundesu yo ne<
again American-States meeting have is (E) (PF)

hachigatsu goro ni>
August around (TFN)
.</td></tr>
<tr><td>Shimizu</td><td>deshoo ne< honto ni jitsu no reberu no yatsu
is (presumptive) (PF) truly real (P) level (P) one

o yarun deshoo ne:<
(D) do is (presumptive) (PF)
.</td></tr>
<tr><td>Shimizu</td><td>ko- kondo no- nanka daburu ne> dakedo ne>
ne- nexti-time (P) somehow overlap (PF) however (PF)</td></tr>
<tr><td>Tanaka</td><td>e<
hm?</td></tr>
<tr><td>Shimizu</td><td>daburimasu ne<
overlap (PF)</td></tr>
<tr><td>Tanaka</td><td>daburimasu ne:<
overlap (PF)</td></tr>
<tr><td>Shimizu</td><td>jijitsu teki ni wa ne:< ikkagetsu mo
actual like in (T) (PF) one-month as-much-as

sa ga arutte koto ni naru to< datte:-
difference (S) have come-about-that (QU) so

omoundesu ne<
think (PF)
.</td></tr>
<tr><td>Tanaka</td><td>daburu ka mo shiremasen> ne<
overlap might (PF)</td></tr>
</table>

Ikeda   mm>
         mhm

{2.55}

Tanaka   kondo   nyuu yooku ni   ikarerundeshitakke<
          next-time New York (TO) go (wonder)

.

Shimizu   n>
           mhm

Tanaka   kono mae<
          this before
          [
Ikeda   n>   n>   kono mae<
         mhm mhm this before
                     [
Shimizu   kono mae nyuu yooku>
                     this before New York
                                        [
Ikeda   kono mae nyuu
                                        this before New
         yooku ja nakattand'su ka<
         York was not (Q)
              [
Tanaka   a kono mae dattand'su ka<
              oh this before it was (Q)

.

Tanaka   sosuto:<
          so-then

{2.45}

TRANSLATION

Tanaka   This talk is completely different, but next time there is going to be a regional meeting around August.

.

Shimizu   I guess so, I guess they are going to do one at a real serious level.

.

Shimizu   The next one is going to overlap though, huh?

Tanaka   Hm?

Shimizu   It'll overlap, huh.

Tanaka   It'll overlap, yeah.

Shimizu   In reality, I guess they'll be as much as a month apart (between the last regional meeting and the upcoming one).

.
Tanaka Yeah, they might overlap.

Ikeda mhm

{2.55}

Tanaka You're going to New York for the next one, right?

.
Shimizu uhuh

Tanaka Or the last one.
[
Ikeda Yeah, yeah, the last one
[
Shimizu The last one was in New York.
[
Ikeda Wasn't the last one in New York?
[
Tanaka Oh the last one was.

.
Tanaka So the:n

{2.45}

Example 4.4 shows that the Japanese officers exchange turns rapidly, with much overlapping talk. This differs sharply form the American example (Example 4.3) of a monological turn with almost no overlapping talk. The rapid exchanges which occur in the Japanese topic supports Hayashi's (1988) finding that Japanese use "sync talk" more frequently than Americans. She claims:

> American speakers create much less sync talk, as they are more conscious of the interactional rule of "one speaker at a time" compared to Japanese speakers. Therefore American speakers' simultaneous talk often occurs in competition to gain the floor. (p. 286)

Most likely the "Americans" in her study were "Anglos" or "White Christian Americans" as Tannen's (1984a) study shows that Jewish Americans frequently use sync talk, or "overlap" as a device for creating rapport. Both Hayashi (1988) and Okazaki (1990) note how Japanese conversationalists perceive such sync talk as supportive behavior in interaction.

The previous analysis of tone-units shown in Table 4.1 further supports the monologic quality of turns in the American meeting, and the rapid, sync talk quality of turn exchange in the Japanese meeting. That is, I showed that although none of the Japanese officers take more than 50 percent of the total number of tone-units in a given topic, all American officers do. Furthermore, two of the officers, Craig and Karen, take more than 80 percent of the total talk-time in each topic. Thus, the American officers present their own topics more monologically than the Japanese.

The difference of monologicality versus frequent and rapid turn-exchange is a feature of the autonomy-interdependence continuum. The American officers focus on each other's autonomy through monologic turns, as the officers-in-charge exhibit their knowledge about their own topics; the Japanese heighten their interdependence through rapid turn-exchange as the group collectively distributes the talk. Strategies for turn distribution are therefore another way in which the American officers satisfy their expectation of within-group independence, and the Japanese respond to their expectation of nonconfrontation.

In sum, the American officers talk most about their own deals; they take the greatest number of tone-units and turns in their own topics which they themselves initiated, use most of their personal talk-time to discuss their own deals, and take long, monologic turns to present topics. In contrast, the Japanese distribute their talk in topics relatively evenly among participants, and across topics, regardless of who originally initiated a topic. The different strategies for talk distribution help both groups accomodate an expected method of interaction: within-group independence for the Americans, and nonconfrontation for the Japanese.

Turn Distribution in a Cross-Cultural Meeting

In the Personnel cross-cultural meeting, both the American officer, Sarah, and Japanese officer, Ito, use their respective turn-distribution strategies. Sarah (40), is the director of personnel, and Ito (59) is the chairman in the same financial institution. In a follow-up conversation with Ito, he reported that the meeting is primarily designed to "fill each other in" on issues relevant to the personnel department on a weekly basis.

Table 4.4 shows the proportional distribution of turns in the 10 topics in the cross-cultural meeting, alongside the topic initiators.

TABLE 4.4
PROPORTIONAL DISTRIBUTION OF TURNS PER TOPIC IN THE PERSONNEL CROSS-CULTURAL MEETING

Meeting	Topic	Proportional Distribution of Tone-Units	
		Ito	*Sarah*
1	Lisa's Law Suit	*33.33	66.67
2	Resumes	*62.50	37.50
3	Contributions	*47.37	52.63
4	Personal Resume (3)	*50.00	50.00
5	Contribution (3)	*33.33	66.67
6	Santa Clara Valley	*54.55	45.45
7	New York	37.50	*62.50
8	BCD	28.57	*71.43
9	Busy Schedules	*60.25	37.50
10	Revised Affirmative Action Plan	33.33	*66.67

The figures in Table 4.4 yield an interesting implication for cross-cultural communication because in using his native strategy, it appears that the Japanese officer, Ito, attempts to distribute turns evenly. This is suggested in the following ways. First, despite the fact that Ito has a substantially greater frequency of topic initiations than Sarah (Ito initiates 70 percent of the topics), Sarah has a greater proportion of turns in more topics than Ito. Second, whereas Sarah has a greater proportion of turns in all of the three topics she initiates, Ito has a greater proportion of turns in only three of the seven topics he initiates. Finally, whereas Sarah has a greater proportion of the turns in three of the seven topics Ito initiates, Ito does not have a greater proportion of the turns in any of the three topics Sarah initiates. Only one topic ("personal resume") has turns that are distributed evenly between the two participants.

In the American meeting, I showed that the officer-in-charge took the highest proportion in his or her own topic; the topic s/he initiated. In contrast, in the Japanese meeting, the officer who initiated a topic did not necessarily have the highest proportion of turns in that topic. As shown above, because Sarah has a greater proportion of turns in all topics she initiates, but Ito has a greater proportion of turns in only three of the seven topics he initiates, in general, it seems that both Sarah and Ito distribute turns following a native pattern.

The use of native strategies in cross-cultural interaction is particularly notable because they account in part for the kinds of negative reactions that are frequently reported. Based on their native assumptions about turn distribution, Japanese may feel that they should be able to freely contribute talk even when topics are other-initiated, but Americans may feel that they should only contribute the majority of their talk to their own topics. The rhythm of talk distribution in cross-cultural communication is then likely to be completely out-of-sync. What each group views as the proper way to distribute talk may therefore be neither meaningful nor comfortable to other parties in cross-cultural communication. Moreover, as I discuss in the following section, participants give meaning to their conversations not only with strategies for distributing topical talk, but also with ways of making relevant points about a topic under discussion.

POINT MAKING

As the "stuff" of topical talk, differences in strategies for making topical points result in mutual suspicion among cross-cultural participants; "Why are they talking about this?"; "How is this relevant?" Previously, I showed that each American officer autonomously delivered his or her own deal, but that the Japanese developed their topical talk interdependently. I then suggested that both these strategies were intraculturally meaningful ways of distributing topical talk. Because such meaning is constructed in culturally sensitive styles of organization, in this section, I illustrate how the American and Japanese officers make points about a topic according to different systems of organization.

Furthermore, conversationalists talk about a topic by contributing a point in a particular way because they want to convey an idea that they feel is relevant to the topic. However, I argue that such "relevance" is colored by cultural expectations; the American and Japanese officers have different strategies for cohering points to a topic, or making intraculturally sensical "on-the-topic" points.

Both groups organize their topical points following the general pattern of topic organization discussed in Chapter 3. That is, the American officers arrange topical points in a linear order; they introduce their first point by stating the present status of the deal, subsequent points by providing background information on the deal, and concluding points by describing plausible outcomes of the deal. The Japanese officers, on the other hand, arrange their points circularly; they make points through examples.

Each strategy responds to culture-specific expectations for interaction. The American officers express their individuality as the officer-in-charge independently states the status and future expectations of the deal. However, to satisfy group understanding of the topic, the officers collectively negotiate the points regarding the background information of the deal, and all officers follow a temporally-organized, linear order of point making. Such aspects of the American point-making strategy then help the officers accomplish within-group independence. The Japanese fulfill their expectation of nonconfrontation, as the circular organization of points allow the officers to shift talk-accountability from themselves to an example.

The American Strategy

In the American meeting, all officers—Craig, Karen and Lynn—organize their points in a linear and temporally-sequenced order. This point-making strategy contains the following steps: a) report the present status of the deal, b) provide background information on the deal, c) provide options about future plans for the deal, and/or d) supply specific expectations about what will eventually happen to the deal. Thus, through rotation, each of the officers-in-charge reports what he or she knows about a deal, discusses its relevant background, and then concludes with a provision of future options. This general pattern is followed by all participants in the American meeting, as I show in the following set of examples.

To commence their line of sequential points, each officer-in-charge first follows their own topic openings with an initial point about the present status of the deal. Example 4.5 shows the initial points.

Example 4.5

Topic	*Officer-in-Charge*	*First Point Following Topic Opening*
Morrow	Craig	we are in< , ah final documentation<
Courtney	Craig	it's in documentation for the first< , THREE of our buyers>

Phelps	Craig	the negotiations for documentation, will begin next week>
Brentnall	Karen	[Brentnall] has mixed reviews on the marketplace>
Garrison	Karen	that's the one that we sold out of a couple of weeks ago<
Hinkley	Lynn	there are so many< hidden< , h- ah: , hidden aspects to the deal< that are not in th- in the projections>

In Example 4.5, the initial points for each topic show how the deals vary in complexity and stage of development. The nature of the topics range from Craig's Morrow deal, the deal that is both simplest and closest to completion, to Lynn's Hinkley deal, with the "many hidden aspects." These points therefore reflect the organization of topics described in Chapter 3: The deals in the American meeting are organized from ones where the future outcome is best known to ones where the future outcome is least known. Furthermore, as the officers make their own initial point about the present status of a deal, they reassert their "in-charge" status following their own topic opening, and thus, emphasize their individuality.

Following a statement about their own deal, each officer-in-charge then gives some background information about the deal. As they give the context for their deals, they begin to move backward along a time-line to show how the deal developed to its present status. Unlike the first point which is always singularly stated by the officer-in-charge, these points are frequently negotiated, as other participants help coconstruct the background. Example 4.6 shows an example of how Lynn helps Craig supply the background information to the "Courtney" Deal. In this point, the two officers jointly determine the portion of the deal that Craig has sold.

Example 4.6

Craig	at this point< I have sold> , uh: I want to say thirty< 't see< ten of fifteen< , and- fifteen< , thirty five [
Lynn	thirty five<
Craig	million>

As Lynn presumably calculates more quickly, she inserts "thirty five" into Craig's point about the Courtney deal. Either through his own calculations or repeating Lynn's, Craig also concludes that he has sold "thirty-five million" of the deal thus far. In the exchange shown in Example 4.6, Lynn therefore supports Craig's point about how his deal has faired in the marketplace. Such coconstruction of a point often occurs in the interim points that have to do with the background of the deals. The American officers therefore also satisfy their need for collectivity by jointly negotiating points about the background of a deal.

Following the background context, the officers then project into the future, and discuss expectations about the final outcome of the deals. As shown in Example 4.7, the officer-in-charge always makes these final points about future expectations.

Example 4.7

Morrow	Craig	I mean **hopefully** I would know something by Friday>
Courtney	Craig	**hopefully**< , those uh: participation agreements will go out this WEEK<
Phelps	Craig	it's **expected** that that will NOT be an extremely long process>
Brentnall	Karen	I **anticipate** that we WOULD be asked if we could sell it without fees>
Garrison	Karen	**HOPEfully**< they will buy by noon today> that's- by noon California time today> . if they DON'T> ah:< , i- i- have< , **hopefully** another buyer in my- pocket<
Hinkley	Lynn	we're just **expecting** a lot of- it's just going to be a lot of work>

Example 4.7 shows that each officer expresses their tentative expectations about the future outcome of the deal by using conditional expressions such as "hope," "expect," and "anticipate." If such future anticipations are predictable or known, the officers also state a time-frame for accomplishment: "by

Friday"; "by the end of this week"; "by noon today." Thus, the American officers systematically make a final point about future expectations of the deals by expressing their hopes and anticipations.

To make their points, the American officers thus move along a time-line; they begin in the present by stating the current status of the deal, move back in time to discuss past developments which provide the background to the deal, and then finally project out to the future to hypothesize plausible outcomes of the deal. The time-line therefore follows a linear organizational pattern: *PRESENT-PAST-FUTURE.* Corresponding to the linear organization of topics in general, then, the American officers organize their points from best known to least known; the present status of the deal is best known, aspects of the events which led to the present circumstances less known, and future possibilities for the deal still even less known.

I have noticed that weather forecasts on the evening news are often reported using the *PRESENT-PAST-FUTURE* temporal order. Weather forecasters frequently report the present temperature and weather conditions, then describe/show the earlier weather conditions of the day, or what the weather was like on the same day in a previous year. Finally, they forecast the weather for several upcoming days.

The *PRESENT-PAST-FUTURE* pattern is followed in each topic, however, the final two constituents, past and future, are repeated until all participants feel that they have fully "talked through" all aspects of the deal, and understood its position in the market. The *PAST-FUTURE* pair is therefore repeated until a projection of a speculation does not warrant further discussion. A typical sequence of this pair proceeds as in the following. If an officer-in-charge makes a point about the future outcome of a deal before other officers feel that they are fully informed, a non-officer-in-charge often asks a question to which the officer-in-charge then supplies further background information.

For example, in an interim point in the Courtney Deal, Craig expresses a future expectation about a buyer interested in the deal: "we'll just have to see how that shakes out." Karen, presumably needing more information, then asks, "are they committed to us, that bank?" to which Craig replies "no." This exchange is shown in Example 4.8.

Example 4.8

Craig — but th- th- the commitment< unfortunately< I think- will be pending< , a favorable< resolution< of the issue over selling assignments non per rata> , **so we'll have to see how that- shakes out**> , uhm<
[
Karen — **are they committed to us**< **that bank**<

Craig — no> uh: Cheryl< feels< that what they will DO< , is get their commitment and then SHOP>

The officers therefore supply background information about the deal, either following an initial point that states the status of the deal, or following a provisional point about future expectations. The final point however, always forecasts the prospects of the deal. Talk-ownership as expressed through point-making is therefore a subset of topic ownership: Each officer delivers the first and final points individually. As the American officers establish individuality in this way, they also complement it with the collective mediation of interim points. Furthermore, because all points follow the same pattern of linear organization, the participants also achieve group understanding. The American point-making strategy thus also helps the officers achieve within-group independence.

The Japanese Strategy

In contrast, the three participants in the Japanese meeting—Tanaka, Ikeda, and Shimizu—use examples to make topical points. Markers such as "*tatoeba*" ("for example"), ."... *mitai na*" ("like"), "*aa yuu/soo yuu/to yuu* (*yoo na*)" ("that kind of/(things) like (that)"), and "*to ka*"("for example"/"et cetera"/"or something") signal these exemplified points, and occur in the Japanese conversation 35 times. This contrasts sharply with the usage of exemplification markers in the American meeting; There are only two uses of "or something" and no uses of "for example" "kind of/something (like)" or "(things) like (that)." Furthermore, as opposed to the temporally sequenced points of the American meeting, the exemplified points are not arranged in a particular linear order; rather, they are arranged circularly to cohere to the general topic under discussion.

The exemplified points come in varying lengths; the shortest is five tone-units and the longest is fifty-two tone-units. Although the longer tone-unit exemplifications are those generally referred to in the literature as narratives, I considered the use of narratives-in-conversation as one type of exemplified point-making. As Polanyi notes (1985:187), "speakers tell stories in conversation to make a point to transmit a message, often some sort of moral evaluation or implied critical judgement about the world the teller shares with other people."

The following excerpt illustrates Ikeda's use of an exemplified point that occurs in a subtopic of "Work and Vacations." Ikeda raises an example to make a point about the subtopic which concerns the different attitudes that Americans and Japanese have toward balancing work and vacations. The excerpt begins as Tanaka remarks that Japanese business people have more pressure from their clients to "entertain" than Americans. These "entertainments" are called "*settai*" and are part of being an employee in a Japanese firm. As Harris and Morgan (1987:391) point out, it is often in such *settai* that "real [Japanese] business and political deals are concluded." The activities of these entertainments range from receptions and dinners to golf rounds, and take up an enormous amount of the businessmen's time. Many evenings and weekends are spent on *settai*; times away from the families; times that might be considered "personal time" by their American counterparts.

Following Tanaka's remark about *settai* (entertainments), Ikeda makes a point about how an American accountant plans to take a vacation despite an urgency of attention called by a bad account. Example 4.9 shows how the exemplification markers "*tatoeba*" ("for example"), "*aa yuu*" ("that kind of"), "*soo yuu*" ("that kind of") and "*to yuu*" ("kind of") surround this exemplified point.

Example 4.9

Tanaka okyaku kara no puresshaa tte anmari nai wake
clients from (P) pressure (T) not-much (NEG) reason

desu yo ne< tokoro ga NIKKEI
is (PF) (PF) however JAPANESE (overseas Japanese businessmen who have Japanese clients)

wa mechakucha okyaku kara no puresshaa mo arun
(T) absurdly clients from (P) pressure also have

desu yo ne<
is (PF) (PF)

.

Ikeda datte **tatoeba** ne< sono:: saikin waruku natta
but **for example** (PF) uh::m recently bad became

kureditto: no banku miitingu de mo ne< , sono:: ma>
credit: (P) bank meeting (L) also (PF), uh::m well

kureditto ga yoosuru ni waruku natten dakara
credit (S) in-other-words bad has-become so

sootoo kinkyuusei ga aru<- miitingu da to omoun
considerably urgency (S) have- meeting is (Q) think

dakeDO:< soko de **tatoeba**: yatotteru ne< ano:: sii
bU:t there (L) **for exa:mple** employed(PF) uh::m C

pii eii: ga desu ne> jibun wa: nekusuto uiikusu ga
P A: (S) is (PF) (him)self (T) next week (S)

bakeishon da to> , de tsuite wa ne< sono< ,
vacation is (Q) , and then following (T) (PF) that
[

Tanaka [warau]

Ikeda repooto no teishutsu ga< , e: okuremasu to> ,
report (P) submission (S) , uh:m will-be-late (Q) ,

sono kekka> , **aa: yuu** hara- happyoo o
that result , **tha:t-kind-of** annou- announcement (D)

suru to ne< , sono: rigaikankeisha de aru:
do (Q) (PF) , uh:m interested-parties who a:re

ginkoodan: wa ne< , nanto naku nattoku
banking grou:ps (T) (PF) , some-how consent

Ikeda shichau to>
do (unfortunately) (Q)

.

Ikeda soide:: u:: **soo yuu no** wa chotto nihon:
so the::n uh::m **that-kind-of thing** (T) a-little Japa:n

ja kangaerare nai>
(L) (T) heard-of (NEG)

{2.75}

Ikeda **to yuu**<
(Q) **kind-of**

.

Ikeda	inshoo	o	mottan	desu	kedo	ne<
	impression	(D)	held	is	but	(PF)

TRANSLATION

Tanaka (They) [Americans] don't have a lot of pressure from their customers [emphatic]. However (those who have) [are in charge of] JAPANESE (clientele) have an incredible amount of pressure from their customers too [emphatic].

.

Ikeda Yeah, but **for example**, uhm even in bank meetings which discuss credits that have recently turned bad, uhm well, in other words the credit has gotten bad so (I) think it's a pretty urgent meeting but, **for example** the CPA hired there, uhm (just says) that (he) is taking a vacation next week, and then, following that, (he says)

[

Tanaka [laughs]

Ikeda the presentation of the report is, ah going to be late, and the result of that, when **that kind of** announcement is made, uhm the concerned banking groups, somehow just kind of accept (it).

.

Ikeda and then uhm **That kind of thing** is unheard of in Japan.

{2.75}

Ikeda That's **the kind of**

.

Ikeda impression (I) got, but

Example 4.9 shows that Ikeda actually makes two points about the subtopic of "American and Japanese attitudes toward work and vacation-taking." Each point contributes to the subtopic in a decreasing level of generality, so that the second, more specific point about the accountant is embedded in the first point about how Americans often handle bad accounts. Furthermore, each point is flanked by markers which signal the level of the exemplified point. The point about the accountant is presignaled with the marker "*tatoeba*" (for example) and postsignaled with "*aa yuu*" (that kind of). The point about the "bad accounts" which encompasses the more specific point about the accountant is further pre- and postsignaled with the markers "*tatoeba*" (for example) and "*soo yuu*" (that kind of). Finally, to exit from the example, Ikeda brings the level of generality back to the subtopic with a long pause of almost three seconds, followed by a comment containing an exemplification marker: "*to yuu* inshoo o mottandesu kedo ne" ("that's **the kind of** impression (I) got." Ikeda therefore marks both the beginning and ending of his example at several levels of generality.

Figure 4.1 illustrates these points along with their markers in terms of four concentric circles. At the nucleus is the most specific point about "the accountant." This point is circumscribed by the point about "bad accounts." The two outermost spheres are the subtopic of "attitudes," and main topic of "work and vacations" respectively.

Figure 4.1 shows how Ikeda arranges his exemplified points circularly, with varying levels of specificity.

Moreover, in addition to indicating the level of specificity, the exemplification markers "*aa yuu*" (that kind of) and "*soo yuu*" (that kind of) also signal the perceived distance of the example from the participants in the interaction. That is, in Japanese, "*aa*" (that) and "*soo*" (that) are a part of a lexical class of words called "*ko-*," "*so-*" and "*a-*." Among the three prefixes, a word with the prefix "*ko-*" references an object or conceptual item which is proximally or perceptually closest in distance to the

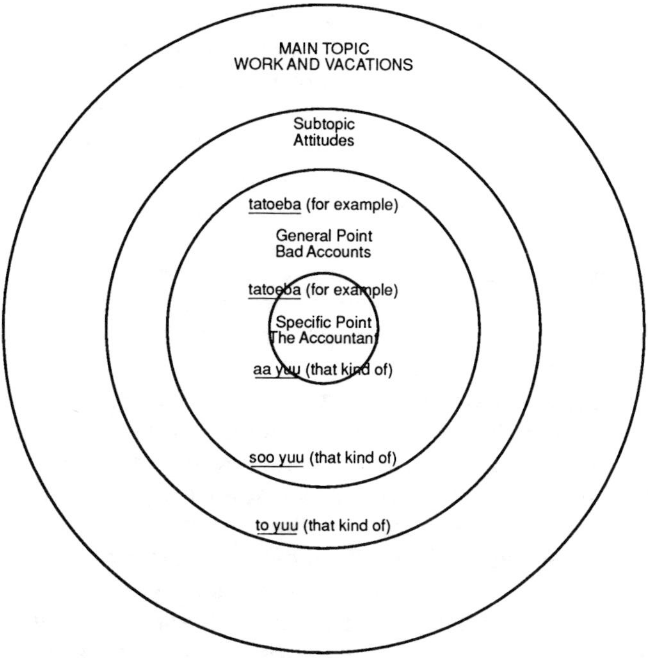

FIGURE 4.1. EXEMPLIFICATION IN JAPANESE POINT MAKING.

interactants; "*so-*," more distant relative to "*ko-*," and "*a-*," still more distant relative to "*ko-*" and "*so-*." (For a more detailed analyses of ko-, so-, and a- words, see, for example, Hosokawa, 1990.) Thus, although both "*aa yuu*" and "*soo yuu*" gloss as "that kind of" in English, in Japanese, an item that is referenced with "*aa*" is perceived as perceptually further away from the participants than one that is referenced with "*soo*." In Example 4.9, then, Ikeda views the specific example about the accountant as more distant from the participants than the more general point about the bad accounts. Hence from Ikeda's point of view, the more specific the example, the more remote from the participants in the interaction.

The other Japanese officers also use a similar pattern to make topical points. For example, Shimizu and Tanaka both use exemplified points in the last topic which concerns Tanaka's proposition to institute the San Francisco Agency. Recall that this is the topic that becomes increasingly confrontational: Tanaka advances his notion that the institution of the Agency as a financial arm to Bank X (the bank in which the officers are employed) is feasible; Shimizu and Ikeda disagree. Example 4.10 shows Shimizu's point of disagreement: if the San Francisco Agency is instituted as a subordinate arm to Bank X, then the employees of the Agency have no incentive for profit. Tanaka then gives a counter-example, his main point being that the rewards of the employees working for the San Francisco Agency do not have to be tied to profit; they can be subsidized by "feeling" (such as extended company care-taking and psychological security in the job, discussed in Harris and Morgan, 1987). Because the "feeling" compensation is an important motivating force behind Japanese employees, Tanaka argues that rather than building in a profit- or commission-based incentive, "feeling" can be used to reward and gain the loyalty of the San Francisco employees.

The excerpt shown in Example 4.10 begins as Shimizu asks a rhetorical and ironic question which indicates his view that instituting the San Francisco Agency is improbable. This point is presignaled with *tatoeba* (for example), and postsignaled with *tte koto* (something like that). Following this point, Tanaka first agrees with Shimizu, then offers his counterpoint: Compensate the employees with a "feeling"-type incentive, rather than by profit. The exemplification markers, *tatoeba* (for example), *tte yuu no* (that kind of thing), *to ka* (things like that) and *sotchi no hoo no* (things of that sort) surround Tanaka's point. Thus,

Shimizu's and Tanaka's exemplifications are also pre- and postsignaled with markers. In Example 4.10 and in future examples, back-channels in the English translation are placed in approximate locations.

Example 4.10

Shimizu sore wa:< , soo suru to> doo yatte kaiketsu suru no<
that (T): , so-do-then how do resolve do (PF)
[
Tanaka ia
well

dakara sore wa<
so that (T)
[
Shimizu shuueki no> tokoro no> , sore jaa
profit (P) place (P) , so-then

tatoeba ashikase o hazushite [warainagara]
for example shackles (D) take-off [laughing]

yaru shika nai **tte koto**> nano<
do-for (them) nothing-else (T) **thing** is-it
[
Tanaka nma:< a: **soo yuu**
we:ll uh:m **that-kind-of**

koto> ni na''n desu yo ne<
thing become is (PF) (PF)
[
Shimizu [warainagara] sore wa
[laughing] that (T)

muri desu yo<
impossible is (PF)

Tanaka ma muri> desu kedo ne<
well impossible is but (PF)
[
Shimizu nn>
mhm

Tanaka ia muri desu kedo:< **tatoeba** sore ga:<
well impossible is bu:t **for example** that (S):

sono:< san furanshisko eijenshii dekite desu ne:< ,
uh:m San Francisco Agency make is (PF): ,
[
Shimizu nn>
mhm

Tanaka sore ga:< koko to ittai ni nareba desu ne:< ,
that (S): here with in-a-body become-if is (PF): ,
[
Shimizu n>
mhm

Tanaka karera no **tatoeba** shuueki **tte yuu no**
their (P) **for example** profit (T) **that-kind-of thing**

wa:< , fuiiringu **to ka** **sotchi no**
(T): , feelings **things-like-that that-way** (P)

hoo **no** shuueki- de-< tottagereba ii wake
direction (P) profit- (U) get-for-if good reason

desu yo ne:<
is (PF) (PF):
[
Shimizu n>

TRANSLATION

Shimizu so then, so then How do you solve (that problem)?
[
Tanaka well so that
[
Shimizu So are you then saying **something like**, **for example**, all (you) can do is [laughing] release them from (their) shackles, from that part of (their) profit?
[
Tanaka Well, uhm (it's) **something like that** [emphatic], yeah.
[
Shimizu [laughing] That's impossible [emphatic].

Tanaka Well it's impossible, but, **for example**, that uhm if the
[
Shimizu mhm
Tanaka San Francisico Agency is instituted, and (it) becomes
[
Shimizu mhm
Tanaka one with (this organization), (we) can give (them)
[
Shimizu mhm

Tanaka their profit say **for example**, in the form of a "feeling," or **some kind of** profit of that sort [emph].
[
Shimizu mhm

As Examples 4.9 and 4.10 show, all three participants signal their exemplified points with verbal markers.

The exemplified points serve the Japanese expectation of nonconfrontation in the following ways. First, an example shifts the responsibility of an opinion from a participant to the example; if a participant is held to the viewpoint expressed in an example, s/he could say, "it's not necessarily my point of view." Furthermore, because an example is an instance of one of many other alternatives, the participants can make the claim that their point is "just an example"; "*tatoeba no hanashi da*" (literally, "it's a for example's talk"). Because a specific opinion cannot be tied to a particular participant, the Japanese conversationalists do not have to be held accountable for the negatively viewed talk.

The shifting of accountability is particularly useful when highly personal points are made in potentially confrontational topics. This is the case in both excerpts illustrated above. In Example 4.9, Ikeda discusses an instance of an accountant who, in his opinion, is about to be negligent by ignoring an account that has gone bad. His metapoint is, then, that the American attitude toward work and vacation-taking (which is different from the Japanese attitude) is *irresponsible;* they take vacations even in urgent situations. Realizing that his viewpoint may not be readily accepted by the other two officers, Ikeda makes his point through an example. (As it turns out, neither Tanaka nor Shimizu agree with Ikeda.) However, the origination of the viewpoint is recast to the example, thus, Ikeda does not have to assume liability.

In Example 4.10, Tanaka and Shimizu also realize that neither is in agreement with the other. Through their examples, Tanaka and Shimizu can express their disagreement about each other's opinions rather than directly accuse one another as stated explicitly through talk. In fact, the talk itself shows Tanaka's agreement; he supports Shimizu's view that the institution of the San Francisco Agency is impossible (*muri*) by agreeing, "*soo yuu koto ni na''n desu yo ne*" ("(it's) something like that"), and then by repeating Shimizu's comment, "*muri desu*" (it's impossible). Only then does he give his counterexample "*kedo, tatoeba*" ("but, for example"). Thus, by shifting the responsibility from themselves to an example, the Japanese officers can make highly personal points without being directly liable. Exemplified point-making is, then, a strategy that allows participants to make personal points nonconfrontationally.

Moreover, the officers further shift the accountability of the viewpoint from themselves to an example by eliding the subject, a commonly used linguistic feature in Japanese. (For more on ellipsis in Japanese, see for example, Hinds, 1980, 1982; S. Maynard, 1985, 1989; Shibamoto, 1984.) In Example 4.9, Ikeda ends his example by eliding the subject "I"; instead of saying "I think the American attitude toward work and vacations is irresponsible," he refers back to the example and says, "that's the IMPRESSION (I) got" ("*to yuu inshoo o mottandesu kedo ne*"). Similarly, in Example 4.10, rather than directly accuse Tanaka by saying "so are YOU saying that," Shimizu elides the subject "you" with the rhetorical questions "*sore wa, soo suru to doo yatte kaiketsu suru no? shuueki no, tokoro no, sore jaa tatoeba ashikase o hazushite yaru shika naitte koto nanno?*" ("How do you solve (that problem)? Are (you) then saying that for example, all (you) can do is release them from (their) shackles, from that part of (their) profit?"). The exemplification markers and elided subjects therefore avert a directly confrontational uptake, as they signal the shift away from the talk to an example.

Another signal in the context of these potentially confrontational points is the use of lengthened sounds (vowels, aspirants, and nasals in decreasing order of frequency). As the officers become aware of the possibly controversial nature of these points, they draw their talk out with such hesitation markers, which occur together with filled pauses and silent pauses. Example 4.11 shows the English translation of the excerpts from Examples 4.9 and 4.10 above, with (~) indicating the approximate location of lengthened sounds.

Example 4.11

TRANSLATION OF EXAMPLE 4.9
"American Accountants and Bad Accounts"

Ikeda Yeah, but for example, uhm ~ ~ even in bank meetings which discuss credits that have recently turned bad, uhm ~ ~ well, in other words the credit has gotten bad so (I) think ~ it's a pretty urgent meeting but ~, for example ~ the CPA ~ hired there, uhm (just says) that (he) is taking a vacation next week, and then, following that, (he says) the presentation of the
[
Tanaka [laughs]

Ikeda report is, ah ~ going to be late, and the result of that, when that ~ kind of announcement is made, uhm ~ the banking groups ~ (who are ~ concerned somehow just kind of accept (it).

.

Ikeda and then ~ ~ uhm ~ ~ That kind of thing is unheard of in Japan ~.
{2.75}
That's the kind of

.

Ikeda impression (I) got, but

.

TRANSLATION OF EXAMPLE 4.10
"The San Francisco Agency"

Shimizu so then ~, so then How do you solve (that problem)?
[
Tanaka well so that
[
Shimizu So are (you) then saying something like, for example, all (you) can do is [laughing] release them from from (their) shackles, from that part of (their) profit?
[
Tanaka Well ~, uhm ~ it's something like that [emphatic], yeah.
[
Shimizu [laughing] That's impossible [emphatic].

Tanaka Well it's impossible, but ~, for example, that ~ uhm ~ if
[
Shimizu mhm

Tanaka the San Francisico Agency is instituted, and (it)
[
Shimizu mhm

Tanaka becomes ~ one with (this organization), (we) can give
[
Shimizu mhm

Tanaka (them) their profit say ~ for example, in the form of a "feeling," or some kind of profit of that sort [emph].
[
Shimizu mhm

In both of these situations, Ikeda's and Tanaka's views are not those held by the majority; there are two officers who disagree.

Thus, as each becomes increasingly aware of their antagonistic position, they begin to draw out their talk. Such "stretch-talk" is therefore another way in which the officers indicate potentially confrontational viewpoints.

At another level, however, because the examples are about experiences with which all participants can identify, the group can focus on the sharedness of the experience portrayed in the example. In Example 4.9, because all officers have dealt with American businessmen, in one sense Tanaka and Shimizu can empathize with Ikeda's point of view. In Example 4.10, Tanaka understands the workings of the profit-incentive, as does Shimizu the Japanese "feeling-incentive." The sharedness conveyed in the experience of these points, then, unites the group in nonconfrontational interaction.

Moreover, as was the case with the larger organization of topics, the Japanese organize their points circularly. That is, the Japanese officers can raise points in any order as long as they cohere nonconfrontationally to the topic. A point in the Japanese meeting, then, need not necessarily be mentioned. This differs from the American point-making strategy; if an officer does not discuss the present status of a deal, the background of a deal, or future forecasts, they appear as if they have omitted critical points in the linear order. Thus, linearity and circularity are different ways of organizing points, and each method of organization meets the American and Japanese expectations for interaction.

Japanese authors often use exemplified points in English writing. For example, to illustrate how seldom Japanese talk in interaction, Doi (1982:219) begins his point with: "One more example to prove the point." In the same article, he later notes the ambiguous quality of Japanese point-making in conversations, and remarks that: "[Japanese] can go on for hours, even gracefully, without coming to the point" (Doi, 1982:221), in part because as M. Matsumoto (1988) notes, explicit and logical articulation of a point is discouraged in the Japanese culture. Conversely, as I discussed in Chapter 1, Hinds (1983) informs us that a diversion from the main point is part of the writing structure. This contrasts with what Tannen (1984b:3) describes as the predominant "stick to the point" or "get to the point" focus of the Western literate tradition.

In short, my point here is not that Americans do not make points by giving examples, as Polanyi (1989) has clearly shown that Americans tell stories (a kind of example) to make a point.

Rather, in an encounter such as a meeting, the primary focus of Americans is to run through the business at hand, and there is little time in such an agenda for examples of any sort. The Americans therefore present their points in a "stick-to-the point" linear order, while at the same time trying as much as possible to preserve the integrity of each officer-in-charge within the bounds of the group. The Japanese, on the other hand, focus on their nonconfrontational interaction as "off-the-topic," exemplified points draw the focus away from rigorous "business-like" talk. The American and Japanese point-making strategies therefore reflect the different ways in which the two groups relate to one another in group-internal business meetings.

CONCLUSION

In summary, the American officers-in-charge talked most about their own deals by individually delivering the initial and final points in them. However, in the interim points, they negotiated an understanding by explaining the deal to other participants if necessary. Furthermore, because all participants sequenced topical points in the same linear order, individual topic delivery is both respected and understood by the group. In conjunction with the findings of Chapter 3, then, the American officers express their expectation of within-group independence as each and every officer is given the right to begin and carry out his or her own topics through to the end. In contrast, the Japanese officers distributed their talk relatively evenly, and arranged exemplified points in a circular organization. As did the opening and shifting strategies, the exemplified points drew the participant focus toward an example. These examples helped unite the Japanese officers in the sharedness of the experience illustrated in the example, and disperse talk-accountability in confrontational talk. Thus, the Japanese officers achieve their expectation of nonconfrontation as they collectively open, deliver, and shift topics, and continually draw the attention away from explicit talk.

As another source of cross-cultural misunderstandings, however, differences in strategies for managing topical talk in business meetings lead to the oft-heard stereotypes: "Japanese are simply illogical, they make all these irrelevant and tangential points''; ''Americans are aggressive, they tirelessly make exhorbitantly logical points.'' Among others, De Mente (1989) and March (1988) warn American businessmen against using Western logic in Japan; ''Beware of using logic'' (De Mente, 1989:127) they say. Similarly, Graham and Sano (reported in Pfeiffer, 1989) warn Japanese businessmen that Americans simply go through items of the business-at-hand, and do not bother to establish a good environment for interrelating. Thus, as these intercultural specialists forewarn, topic-management strategies that seem meaningful and useful in intracultural communication sometimes create problems in cross-cultural interaction.

CHAPTER 5

FINDING THE PLACE TO EXPRESS SUPPORT: BACK-CHANNELS

Japanese are overly accommodating and inscrutable.

Americans are unattentive and selfish.

In intracultural relationships, both Americans and Japanese have ways to demonstrate support; however, they differ in their strategies for its expression. This is because the meaning of supportive behavior varies; it entails different perspectives about the degree of explicitness with which to communicate support, as well as different expectations about the time and the place of its articulation. For example, Jameson and Schoenberger (1988) describe an incident where an executive of a Japanese automobile company thinks support should be expressed among co-workers through intense and intimate bonding, by going out to have beers at the end of the day. Instead, he finds that the American employees go home at five o'clock to be with their families, or go out with "buddies," with friends external to the company.

Americans and Japanese therefore have different ideas about the appropriate contexts in which to express their support in social relationships. In Chapter 2, following Bennett and Ishino (1963), Fruin (1983), Kondo (1990), and Nakane (1970), I described the intensity of personal ties through which male,

Japanese employees relate to one another. In contrast, I discussed the division of business and personal lives of Americans; unlike the Japanese who view the "company as family," Kondo (1990), De Mente (1989), Martin (1990) and Nakane (1970) among others describe how Americans separate their relationships at work from other relationships of a more intimate sort. It is not surprising, then, that the overt expression of support is considerably greater among Japanese employees than among American ones.

The different ways of voicing support among Americans and among Japanese lead to a mismatch of expectations in cross-cultural business conversations; the end product, as De Mente (1989), Graham and Sano (reported in Pfeiffer, 1988), Harris and Morgan (1987) and Thian (1988) point out, is often negative judgments. Americans who expect to "get down to business" frequently find Japanese support behavior overly accommodating. "Why do they keep agreeing when they don't really mean it? They just keep saying yes and that's because they are going to pull a sly move. Japanese are inscrutable." On the other hand, Japanese, who expect an overt expression of support perceive Americans as unattentive. "Why are they so indifferent? They don't listen to what you say, and that's because all they do is think about themselves. Americans are *katte* (selfish)."

BACK-CHANNELS AS SUPPORTIVE BEHAVIOR

Until recently, studies have focused primarily on the conversational behavior of the "speaker," however, with the recognition of the need for studying the role of the "hearer" or "listener," scholars have begun to explore the significant role played by the supporter. Moreover, Erickson (1979, 1985) and S. Maynard (1986b, 1989) point out that studies of conversation have focused mostly on the role of the "speaker," relegating the "hearer" to a secondary and passive role. However, Hayashi (1988) and S. Maynard (1989) inform us that "listeners" in Japanese conversation play a primary and active role. Thus, because I view conversation as interactive and dynamic, and participants as simultaneously engaging in leading and supportive roles, I refer to the speaking participant as the "leader"; the others, "supporters." I avoid the terms "speaker," "hearer," or "listener" because of their association with models that presuppose a static, linear speaker-hearer or speaker-listener relationship, wherein there is a speaker and listener/hearer at discrete points in time. Leaders and supporters change roles constantly, and neither one is meaningful without the other.

The comparative study of support behavior is critical not only because its expression is elusive and easily misunderstood in cross-cultural communication, but also because it is inherently metacommunicative; Americans and Japanese both have implicit ways of expressing support. One such implicit expression of support is through the well-recognized "back-channel." In his original conception, Yngve (1970:568) defines the term, "back-channel" as: "the person who has the turn receives short messages such as 'yes' and 'uh-huh' without relinquishing a turn."

In addition to the many studies of back-channels in English (for example, Erickson and Shultz, 1982; Gumperz, 1982a; Tannen, 1984a), Clancy (1982), S. Maynard (1986b, 1988, 1989) and Szatrowski (1989) have studied back-channels in Japanese, and LoCastro (1987), S. Maynard (1986b, 1989), and White (1989) have examined back-channels comparatively in American and Japanese conversation. All comparative studies point to the considerably greater frequency of *aizuchi* (literally, mutual hammering) or back-channels in Japanese conversation than in American conversation.

In this chapter, I compare the back-channel strategies of the American and Japanese officers, and discuss their implications in cross-cultural meetings. I show that the Americans and the Japanese have distinct styles for articulating support; they not only use back-channels with different frequencies but in different topical contexts. More specifically, in addition to providing further evidence to the findings of other scholars that Japanese back-channel more frequently than Americans, I show that the supporting officers in the Japanese meeting back-channel frequently in the context of topical points to meet their expectation of nonconfrontation. In contrast, the supporting officers in the American meeting follow topic openings with back-channels to acknowledge topic ownership and the in-charge status of individual officers. Furthermore, in the cross-cultural meetings, the Japanese officers accentuate their frequent back-channeling as they not only continue to back-channel more frequently than the Americans, but also back-channel more than they did in the in-group Japanese meeting.

In the present study, I considered back-channels as "little noises of tentative suggestion, understanding and encouragement" (Harris and Morgan, 1987:391), which do not signal supporters' intention of taking a turn. English back-channels in the data included short utterances such as: a) mhm(:), b) u(n)huh, c) ye(a)h, d) ok (latched only), e) (that's) right, and f) I think so. Japanese back-channels included: a) *(u)(:)n(:)(m)(:)*, b) *ee(:)*, c) *ha(i)(:)*, d) *soo (da) (yo) (ne)(:)*, e) *soo (de)su (ka) (ne)(:)*, f) *soo ka mo ne(:)*, and g) *naruhodo (ne)(:)*. (See LoCastro, 1987:108, for a more exhaustive listing of types of back-channels in English and Japanese.)

BACK-CHANNELS IN THE INTRACULTURAL MEETINGS

General Differences in Back-Channel Distributions

In general, there are two major differences in the way back-channels are distibuted in the intracultural meetings. First, substantiating the well-documented finding that Japanese back- channel more than Americans (LoCastro, 1987; S. Maynard, 1986b, 1989; White, 1989), I find that there are more back-channels in the Japanese meeting than in the American meeting. Second, while the Japanese supporters continuously back-channel while they are not speaking, this does not necessarily hold for the American supporters.

Back-Channel Frequencies

The figures in Table 5.1 of total back-channels, back-channel per tone-unit ratios, and back-channel per minute averages, indicate that the Japanese officers back-channel more frequently than the Americans. Back-channel per tone-unit ratios are the total number of back-channels to the total number of tone-units; back-channel per minute averages are the total number of back-channels divided by the number of meeting minutes.

In Table 5.1, the back-channel per tone-unit ratios indicate that the Japanese officers back-channel 1.2 times more fre-

TABLE 5.1
FREQUENCY OF BACK-CHANNELS IN INTRACULTURAL MEETINGS

Meeting	Total Number of Back-Channels	Back-Channel/ Tone-Unit Ratio	Back-Channel Per Minute
American	163	.1614	6.04
Japanese	179	.1998	8.95

quently than their American counterparts; the back-channel per minute averages show that the Japanese back-channel 1.5 times more per minute than the Americans. Supporting the research of other scholars, then, these figures illustrate that the Japanese back-channel considerably more than the Americans.

Supporter Back-Channels and Leader Volubility

An analysis of back-channel distributions across participants shows that in both the American and Japanese meetings, the officer who speaks the least is the officer who back-channels the most. That is, the participant with the lowest number of tone-units has the highest number of back-channels. Table 5.2 shows the number of back-channels by participant, and ranks participants from highest to lowest back-channeler and from most to least voluble.

Table 5.2 shows that, in the American meeting, Lynn is the highest back-channeler, and she speaks the least; in the Japanese meeting, Shimizu is the highest back-channeler, and he also speaks the least. This therefore illustrates how both the American and Japanese supporters show their support to the lead officer by using back-channels.

TABLE 5.2
BACK-CHANNEL AND TONE-UNIT RANKINGS

Meeting	Number of Back-Channels	Back-Channel/ Ranking	Tone-unit Ranking
American			
	81	Lynn	Karen
	54	Karen	Craig
	28	Craig	Lynn
Japanese			
	101	Shimizu	Tanaka
	43	Ikeda	Ikeda
	35	Tanaka	Shimizu

Table 5.2 also points to the direct inverse relationship between the frequency of back-channels and volubility in the Japanese meeting; the more an officer speaks, the less likely he is to back-channel. In the American meeting, however, there is no such relationship; although Karen is generally more voluble than Craig, she also back-channels with almost twice the frequency that he does. Because Maltz and Borker (1982) point out that women back-channel more frequently than men, and since the two highest back-channelers in the American meeting are women, gender may also be a critical variable in determining frequency of back-channels. Thus, the Japanese officers consistently back-channel when they are not speaking, but the American officers do not necessarily back-channel as supporters.

The findings of supporter back-channels and leader volubility have interactional significance because they show that both the American and Japanese supporters strategically use back-channels to express their support of the participant in the lead role. This is because back-channels express a kind of agreement for both groups of officers. They say "Yes, yes, I'm following." However, back-channels can also mean "Yes, I agree with what you are *saying*." This is the level at which the Americans and Japanese appear to differ. That is, because talk content matters little for Japanese, they can liberally use back-channels without it conflicting with their interactional needs; the use of back-channels are in concordance with their expectation of collective and nonconfrontational interaction. Rather, through back-channels, supporters deemphasize talk content, and focus upon interactional agreement for the sake of group unity. But for the Americans, because talk content matters, and because they express individually variant ideas through talk, constant back-channels and a "superficial" expression of agreement is neither necessary nor desirable. Such an expression of agreement may be seen as "false," as it jeopardizes the American respect for the expression of different individual viewpoints. Thus, each group expresses support through different back-channel frequencies to meet their respective interactional needs and expectations.

Topical Contexts of Back-Channels

In the general analysis above, I discussed a similarity in American and Japanese back-channeling strategies; the officers in both meetings back-channel to express their support as the least voluble participant is the highest back-channeler. However, I also discussed the important difference that the Japanese officers back-channel more frequently than the Americans. When the context of back-channels are examined in the conversational context, I find another difference: The American and Japanese officers use back-channels in different topical contexts. That is, the American officers use back-channels in the fuzzy context of topic margins, but the Japanese use back-channels in the context of topical talk.

In order to arrive at this conclusion, I compared back-channel per tone-unit ratios in the meetings overall (shown in Table 5.1) with back-channel per tone-unit ratios in topic margins. (A topic margin extends from the last tone-unit of a final point in a topic to the beginning of a first point in the succeeding topic.) Table 5.3 shows that back-channels occur more frequently in the topic margins of the American meeting than in the Japanese meeting.

According to the figures of the back-channel per tone-unit ratios in Table 5.3, the American officers back-channel more frequently in topic margins than the Japanese. However, because the Japanese officers generally back-channel more frequently, their back-channels occur consistently throughout the topical talk. In the following, I discuss each of these contexts in further detail.

The American Strategy: Back-Channels in Topic Margins

To locate the topical context of back-channels in the intracultural meetings, Table 5.3 showed that the American officers back-channel most frequently in topic margins. Exploring this context further, I find that the specific context in which back-channels recurrently occur is between a topic opening and an initial point of the American officers-in-charge. Back-channels occur in this context in five of the seven topics.

TABLE 5.3
BACK-CHANNEL/TONE-UNIT IN MEETING OVERALL AND IN TOPIC MARGINS

Meeting	Meetings Overall	Topic Margins
American	.1614	.0178
Japanese	.1998	.0134

In the previous two chapters, I described the American strategies for topic opening and point-making. The American officers each opened their own deals by naming them, and individually described the status of the deal in their initial points. Continuing their point-making, the officers-in-charge then described the background of the deals with the help of supporters, and finally made his or her own concluding points about the plausible outcomes of the deal. Sometimes the final two constituents in the pattern of *STATUS-BACKGROUND-OUTCOME* were repeated if more detailed explanations were necessary. In this case, following an officer's premature forecast of future options, supporters asked questions, and officers-in-charge responded. The American officers-in-charge and supporters thus coconstruct an understanding of the deals so that each officer-in-charge feels that s/he has fully explained a deal, and the supporters feel that they have fully understood it.

This "checking" process appears to occur earlier on in the topic, wherein the officer-in-charge always uses short pauses (less than 1 second) following topic openings to "check" the reactions of supporters. The supporters then respond in the following ways. First, supporters may remain silent in which case the officer-in-charge continues with the initial point. Example 5.1 shows Craig's opening of the topic of the Morrow deal, followed by the initial point.

Example 5-1

Craig   all right first deal today is Morrow> , a:nd we are in< , ah final documentation<

The Morrow deal is one of two topics which do not contain a back-channel; the other is the last topic of "Deal Listing." Back-channels do not occur in these topics (first and last topics) most likely because there is little concern for them; Craig's "Morrow" deal is a "done deal"; the "leftover" deals in the final topic do not call for immediate action.

The supporters in the American meeting follow topic openings with back-channels in the remaining five topics. This is because unlike the topics of "Morrow" and "Deal Listing," the decisions made in the meeting concerning the subsequent actions taken for these deals will critically affect their eventual outcome. The supporters therefore need to be informed about the deal before hypothesizing about future options. By following topic openings with back-channels, then, the supporters express the degree to which they are acquainted with the deals. Back-channels that follow topic openings either occur alone, or are followed by a question. Example 5.2 shows how Lynn opens her topic of the "Hinkley" deal, and Karen inserts the back-channel "un-huh" between the topic opening and the initial point.

Example 5-2

Lynn	my deal- Hinkley-, it is a complicated deal> ,
	[
Karen	**UN-HUH**
Lynn	there are so many< hidden< , h- ah: , hidden aspect to the deal< that are not in th- in the projections>

Because the American officers introduce their topics with little information in their "name-the-deal" topic opening, they need a cue to know whether they should provide more information, or continue with the details of the deal. In Example 5-2, back-channels such as Karen's "UN-HUH" is a cue which informs the officer-in-charge that the supporters recognize the topic. Back-channels in the context of *OPENING-INITIAL POINT* then allow an officer-in-charge to continue. In Example 5-2, Karen gives Lynn an emphatic "un-huh" to imply the metamessage: "Yes! Go on, I know what you're talking about." In this way, back-channels which follow topic openings and precede initial points serve the purpose of directing the officer-in-charge about how to present a deal.

On the other hand, if a question or other linguistic cue indicating insufficient information follows the back-channel, it overrules the affirmative acknowledgement response. It says, "No, I don't know about that deal, give me some background." Example 5-3 shows how Craig opens his topic of "the Phelps deal" with a verbal equation, and Lynn back-channels with "mhm" to indicate her recognition of the topic. Karen then also back-channels "mhm," but adds a question to suggest that she needs more information. In Example 5-3, Karen's question is specific; she needs to know whether the Phelps deal is "a primary." Craig responds affirmatively, and then proceeds with the first point of the deal.

Example 5-3

Craig a:nd< the: other deal< that I 'ave started to work on is Phelps< , a:nd<-
[
Lynn **mhm**
[
Karen **mhm**> , that's a primary> right<

Craig that's a primary< 'nd uhm the documentation< , the negotiation for documentation will begin next week>

In Example 5-3, then, Craig pauses to check for topic recognition, and allows Lynn and Karen to indicate the degree to which they are acquainted with the deal. Only after checking for information adequacy indicated by supporters through their "topic acknowledgement back-channels" does Craig continue to talk about his deal. In turn, the use of back-channels following topic openings signals that supporters have adequate information, unless other cues, such as the question in Example 5-3 overrule them.

In short, by responding with back-channels, American supporters inform the officers-in-charge whether they know about the topic based only on the information provided by the name-the deal topic opening. If supporters respond with back-channels following the topic opening, the officer-in-charge continues with the details of the deal; if supporters do not respond with back-channels, or use a questioning cue following a back-channel, the officer-in-charge provides further information, and then continues to discuss the topic in further detail. As the officers-in-charge check for supporter back-channels, and as supporters back-channel, the American officers jointly negotiate the individual contributions of each officer. The back-channels contextualized in the topical locale of openings and initial points therefore satisfy the American interactional expectation of within-group independence as the officers establish rapport among officers before each officer-in-charge is given the autonomy to talk on a topic independently.

The Japanese Strategy: Point Acknowledgment

The supporters in the Japanese meeting follow topic openings with back-channels only once. Instead, the Japanese supporters use frequent back-channels in a different context; they incessantly back-channel in the context of topical points. This partially explains the higher frequency of back-channels in the Japanese meeting than in the American meeting, since there are more points in a given conversation than there are topics, and the American officers place the majority of their back-channels in topic margins.

As described in Chapter 4, the Japanese officers often make topical points through examples. Example 5-4 shows that the Japanese supporters back-channel frequently in the context of these exemplified points. This excerpt is a subtopic of the major topic, "Work and Vacations." Here, Tanaka explains why Japanese expatriates have so much work. He argues in his first, general point that the exorbitant amount of work that these expatriates have results in part because they have Japanese clients who expect to be entertained. This point about entertainment is presignaled with *tatoeba* (for example) and postsignaled with *soo yuu* (that kind of). In his specific point, he gives examples of the kinds of *settai* (entertainment) activities in which the Japanese must participate. These specific examples are again pre- and postsignaled with *to ka* (things like that) and *soo yuu* (things like that). Example 5-4 illustrates 11 back-channels by the supporters, Shimizu and Ikeda, as Tanaka makes his points. (The back-channels in the English translation are placed in approximate positions).

Example 5-4

Tanaka ia nikkei no tantoosha tte
well Japanese clients (P) the-person-in-charge of (T)

yuu no wa< tsumari yasumi DAke ja nakute
say-that (T) in-other-words vacations ONly NEG

desu ne< **tatoeba** settai mo arun desu yo
is (PH) **for example** entertainments also have is (FP)

ne:< , kore de shiten no:< , KANARI no
(FP): , this with branch (P): , CONSIDERABLE (P)
[
Ikeda **m**> **m**>

Tanaka bubun o ne< gorufu da **to ka**> ma<
proportion (D) (PF) golf is things-like-that well
[[
Ikeda **m**>
m>
[
Shimizu **m**> **m**>

Tanaka yoru osoku made ne:< , nomanakya ikenai kara
night late until (PF): , have-to-drink so
[[
Ikeda **m**> **nm:**<

Tanaka **soo yuu** no de tsubusaretemasu kara> ne<
that-kind-of-thing (P) with be-squashed so (PF)
[
Ikeda **nm:**<
[
Shimizu **mm**<

Tanaka taihen desu yo ne< **soo yuu** imi de>
troublesome is (PF) (PF) that-kind-of sense with

Shimizu **mm**>
[
Ikeda **nmm**<

Shimizu **soo da ne**<

TRANSLATION

Tanaka Yeah but in other words for the administrators in charge of Japanese clients, it's not just the vacations, but **for example** they have entertaining to do also, and with this, a LARGE proportion of the, branch
[
Ikeda **mhm mhm**

Tanaka is, (you know), (taken up by) golf **and things like**
[
Ikeda **mhm**

Tanaka **that**, well, (we) have to go drinking until late at
[[
Ikeda **mhm** **yeah**
[
Shimizu **mhm** **mhm**

Tanaka night, so **things like that** take away time, right?
[[
Ikeda **mhm** **yeah**
[
Shimizu **yeah**

Tanaka (It's) a lot of work, in that sense.

Shimizu **yeah**
[
Ikeda **yeah**

Shimizu **Yeah**, (you're) **right**.

Example 5-4 shows that in the general point about *settai* (entertainment), Ikeda back-channels with "*m m*" ("mhm, mhm"). Then, in the context of the specific points about the obligatory golf and drinking activities, Ikeda and Shimizu back-channel seven times. Finally, as Tanaka exits from the more general point about *settai* (entertainment), Ikeda and Shimizu back-channel again three times. The general and specific points, their exemplification markers and the back-channels are shown in Figure 5.1.

As Shimizu and Ikeda back-channel in the context of both the general and specific points, they acknowledge Tanaka's point about how they, as members of a Japanese expatriate community, must participate in entertainments which involve golf and

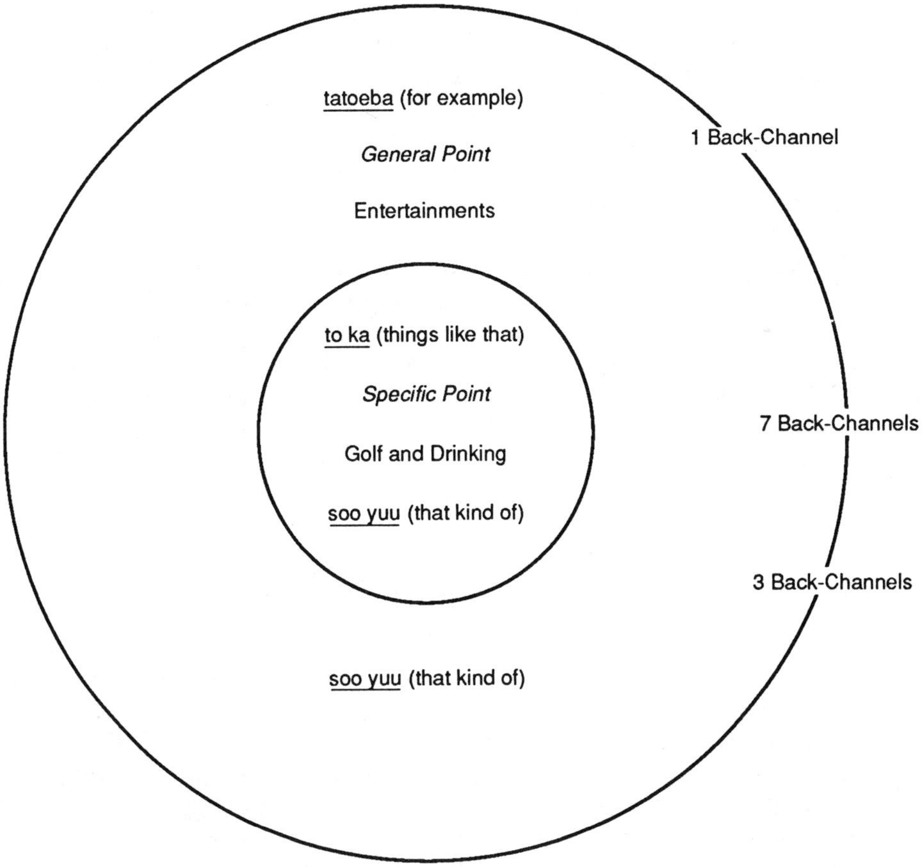

FIGURE 5.1. SUBTOPIC "WE HAVE A LOT OF WORK"

late-night drinking. As the exemplified point draws the focus away from the topic and toward the example, participants therefore commiserate in the common experience portrayed in the example; "Yes, yes," they say, "We have so much work." When the Japanese officers back-channel, then, what they acknowledge is not the point of view voiced by a particular participant, but the commonality of the experience as illustrated in the example. Thus, as Lebra (1987) informs us, it is precisely because the Japanese emphasize relationship over talk-content that Japanese encourage exemplified points through back-channels. Through continuous back-channels which support the insistent focus away from talk, the Japanese supporters actively strengthen their expectation of nonconfrontational interaction.

In sum, both the American and Japanese supporters use back-channels to support leading participants. However, because interactional expectations differ between the two groups, the Americans and Japanese use different back-channel strategies: the Japanese officers back-channel more frequently than the Americans, and they use back-channels in the context of topical talk, while the Americans contextualize theirs in topic margins. Each of these strategies satisfies the respective intracultural expectations for interaction: As the American supporters back-channel between the leading participant's topic opening and initial point, the officers negotiate the right of each officer-in-charge to continue to present the topic independently; as the Japanese officers back-channel in the context of topical points, they collectively share in the experience of the exemplified points.

BACK-CHANNELS AND CROSS-CULTURAL COMMUNICATION

In her description of silence in Japanese communication, Lebra (1987) characterizes back-channels as an intrinsic part of a mode of communication structured through silence. I discussed above that the Japanese effort to preserve their interactional need of nonconfrontation is characterized through their relentless use of back-channels throughout a conversation. In contrast, I showed how the American officers use back-channels more modestly. They tended to place fewer back-channels in a more limited and specific conversational context: in topic margins. Such a difference in supportive behavior can cause problems in cross-cultural communication. As Lebra (1987:344) observes: "the English speaker is annoyed by the Japanese listener uttering *aizuchi* (back-channels) too often, too untimely, and too loudly." They feel patronized, and view the Japanese with suspicion; "What's behind all this?"

The Japanese who are well accustomed to frequent and continual back-channels on the other hand, feel that the American cross-cultural interactants are "not listening" and, therefore, "not understanding." Szatrowski (1989) describes an incident between an American student and a Japanese teacher who repeatedly asks the student the same question. Feeling that the situation was both inappropriate and disagreeable, the student kept thinking, "Why does (this teacher) keep asking ME the same questions over and over again." Then, three days later, the teacher remarked, "You don't back-channel very often, do you. (You) will make Japanese insecure" (Szatrowski, 1989:32, my translations).

In a personal example, I have often stopped short in the middle of a telephone conversation with an American friend, asking suddenly: "Hello?" As I talk to my "silent" friend, a thought runs through my mind, "Maybe the phone went dead." However, quite to the contrary, my friend is "still there," and she responds, "Yeah, what happened?" Although somewhat embarassed, other Japanese friends have consoled me as I recount these experiences to them; they tell me that they too are often overcome with the same insecurity when their friends suddenly seem to disappear at the other end of the line.

Back-channels are therefore an important part of a cultural rhythm in conversation. In the following, I compare American and Japanese back-channel strategies, this time in the two cross-cultural meetings, Personnel and Corporate Banking, used as back-up data. In general, I find that the American officers use the back-channel strategy described earlier of the intracultural American meeting, but that the Japanese officers combine the back-channel strategies found in both intracultural meetings. The combination of supporter strategies is significant not only because it shows how the Japanese officers extend their native habits to the cross-cultural meetings, but also because the combination results in the accentuated use of back-channels.

More specifically, I find the following. First, corroborating

Maynard's (1989:221) finding that Japanese generally tend to "send more frequent back-channels toward American partners," than vice versa, I find that the Japanese supporters back-channel more than their American counterparts, and they do so regardless of who speaks more. Second, both the American and Japanese supporters back-channel following topic openings, but only the Japanese back-channel in the context of topical points. I argue that as the Japanese officers attempt to adjust to the nonnative cross-cultural interaction, they accentuate the use of back-channels by combining native and target-language strategies.

General Differences in Back-Channel Distributions

Several figures indicate that the Japanese supporters in the cross-cultural Personnel and Corporate Banking meetings back-channel more than the Americans. First, Table 5.4 shows each participant's total number of back-channels and their back-channel per tone-unit ratios.

Both sets of figures in Table 5.4 indicate that Japanese back-channel more than Americans in the cross-cultural meetings. In the Personnel Meeting, the Japanese officer Ito back-channels more than the American officer, Sarah; in the Corporate Banking Meeting, the Japanese officers, Tanaka and Ikeda, back-channel more than the American officers, Cindy and Claire.

When the figures in Table 5.4 are combined to form Amer-

TABLE 5.4
BACK-CHANNELS IN CROSS-CULTURAL MEETINGS

Meeting	Participant	Number of Back-Channels	Back-Channel Tone-Unit Ratio
Personnel			
	Ito	255	.2921
	Sarah	158	.1968
Corporate Banking			
	Tanaka	134	.1642
	Ikeda	73	.1916
	Cindy	45	.1206
	Claire	41	.0838

ican and Japanese groups; these figures again show that Japanese back-channel more than Americans. Table 5.5 shows the number of back-channels and the back-channel per tone-unit ratios for the American and Japanese groups.

The figures in Table 5.5 illustrate that the Japanese group back-channels almost twice as frequently (1.89 as frequently) as the American group in terms of the total number of back-channels; almost 1.75 times as frequntly in terms of back-channel per tone-unit ratios.

This finding is particularly significant in light of the fact that in the comparisons of back-channels in the intracultural meetings discussed earlier, the Japanese supporters back-channeled 1.2 times as frequently as the Americans. In the cross-cultural meetings, then, the Japanese officers back-channel with an even greater frequency than the officers in the intracultural Japanese meeting. In other words, the Japanese back-channel strategy is not only extended to use in the cross-cultural meetings, but it is further accentuated in use with cross-cultural participants.

There are several factors likely to contribute to the increased use of back-channels in the cross-cultural meetings. First, frequent back-channels are the conventional way to express support in Japanese interaction (Clancy, 1982; Lebra, 1987; LoCastro, 1987; S. Maynard, 1986b, 1988, 1989; Szatrowski, 1989; White, 1989). The Japanese officers, therefore, use their own back-channel strategy in the cross-cultural meetings because as members of the same banking institution (for both intracultural and cross-cultural meetings), supportive gestures are both desirable and necessary.

Second, there is a power differential between the American and Japanese groups in the cross-cultural meetings. Although all participants are officers, the Japanese hold higher positions than the Americans. Furthermore, the Japanese are all men; the Americans, women. While at first glance, these differences

TABLE 5.5
BACK-CHANNELS OF AMERICAN AND JAPANESE GROUPS IN CROSS-CULTURAL MEETINGS

Participant Group	Number of Back-Channels	Back-Channel/ Tone-Unit Ratio
American	244	.2044
Japanese	462	.3558

may seem as if the American women should back-channel more, as I have described, it turns out to be the contrary. It is plausible that this occurs because the higher-ranking, male Japanese officers continue to seek out their expected mode of interaction: nonconfrontation. Such an interactional style in their view, best promotes a productive and fruitful interaction.

Finally, the Japanese officers are communicating in a non-native language. Second-language communicators view the unfamiliar target-language code and style as not only difficult, but problematic; they are often aware that they must do something different, although they may not be sure exactly what to do differently. The result is an accentuation of the kinds of behavioral and communicative strategies that help in intracultural communication; one of these being frequent back-channels.

How Americans evaluate the extensive use of back-channels by Japanese in cross-cultural communication requires further investigation. However, as I pointed out earlier, Lebra (1987) suggests that the incessant back-channels of Japanese result in annoyance on the part of Americans. An accentuation, then, would only result in further aggravation, as well as in perhaps, a complimentary schismogenesis (Bateston, 1972; Tannen, 1984a): As both groups apply more and more of their native strategies in the cross-cultural encounter, the conversation becomes increasingly assymetrical. Each group then becomes frustrated as efforts to improve communication actually worsens the already problematic situation of differences in interactive styles.

Back-Channel Strategies and Volubility

In the comparison of intracultural meetings, I discussed how the least voluble officers had the highest frequencies of back-channels in both American and Japanese meetings. An analysis of the cross-cultural meetings, however, shows that the least voluble officer is the highest back-channeler only if the participant is a Japanese, or conversely, if the most voluble participant is an American. This is shown in Table 5.6 which ranks the officers in the two cross-cultural meetings from highest to lowest back-channeler, and from most to least voluble.

These rankings show that in the Personnel Meeting, the Japanese officer, Ito, is the higher back-channeler, and is less voluble than the American officer, Sarah. However, in the

TABLE 5.6
RANKING OF OFFICERS IN CROSS-CULTURAL MEETINGS FROM HIGHEST TO LOWEST NUMBER OF BACK-CHANNELS AND TONE-UNITS

Meeting	Ranking According to Back-Channels	Ranking According to Volubility	
			HIGH
Personnel			
	Ito	Sarah	
	Sarah	Ito	
			LOW
			HIGH
Corporate Banking			
	Tanaka	Tanaka	
	Ikeda	Claire	
	Cindy	Cindy	
	Claire	Ikeda	
			LOW

Corporate Banking Meeting, the Japanese officer, Tanaka, is the highest back-channeler *and* the most voluble among the four meeting participants. Thus, although there is an inverse relationship between back-channeling and volubility in the Personnel Meeting, there is no such relationship in the Corporate Banking Meeting. The Japanese participants in the cross-cultural meetings, then, back-channel more than the American officers even when they speak more.

Here, I want to stress the point that supporters play a primary and active role in Japanese interaction. For the Americans, it seems that it is the "quiet" conversationalists who back-channel more as supporters, but for the Japanese, both quiet and talkative interactants back-channel frequently. Thus, the Japanese express their *active* participation through the extensive use of back-channels. However, because back-channels are ambiguously encoded vocalizations, the supporters who use them are often considered to play a passive and secondary role in comparison to the major role played by the "speaker." But for Japanese, it is precisely the ambiguous and polysemic quality of back-channels that make them so useful in nonconfrontational Japanese interaction. Japanese interactants use numerous back-channels as supporters so that they can downplay the unfavorably viewed content of talk, and focus on the primary goal of nonconfrontational Japanese conversation: listenership.

Topical Contexts of Back-Channels

The timing and context of placement of conversational listenership is as critical to cross-cultural communication as its frequency; thus, here, I compare the positioning of American and Japanese back-channels in topics. I show examples of how both the American and Japanese officers use the intracultural American strategy of placing back-channels following topic openings, and how the Japanese officers use their native strategy of back-channeling in the context of topical points. As previously suggested, the combined strategies account in part for the intensified frequency of Japanese back-channeling in the cross-cultural meetings: The Japanese officers back-channel following topic openings, *as well as* in the context of topical points, while the American officers primarily confine their back-channel to the conversational context succeeding topic openings.

The American Strategy

Examples 5-5 and 5-6 illustrate an American and a Japanese officer's use of back-channels following topic openings. First, in the Personnel Meeting, the American officer, Sarah, follows Ito's topic opening with two back-channels of the "mhm" variety. The excerpt in Example 5-5 is taken from a topic about a resume that Ito has received from an associate.

Example 5-5

Ito	and uh:< last one, is s- quite personal> the uh:, you know Kenny> , of the international> bank> , HE just
	[
Sarah	**mhm**<
Ito	gave me> uh: his daughter's, uh:, uh resume>
	[
Sarah	**mhm**<

The American officer, Sarah, therefore uses her native strategy of back-channeling following topic openings. As an illustration of a Japanese officer who back-channels in the same context, Example 5-6 shows an excerpt taken from the Corporate Banking Meeting, a meeting with four participants, and designed to discuss relevant issues of the Corporate Banking

Department on a weekly basis. The excerpt in Example 5-6 begins as an American officer, Claire (45) opens her topic of "File Cabinets." This topic concerns planning for the new organization of file cabinets in the department, following an imminent physical rearrangement of departments in the bank. In the excerpt shown in Example 5-6, Tanaka contextualizes two back-channels "mhm" and "yeah, sure" between Claire's own topic opening and her initial point on the topic.

Example 5-6

Claire uh- f- the file cabinets> , would be the next thing<
[[
Tanaka **mhm**> **yeah**> ,
sure>
[
Claire ok< , uh:m< what we need to decide< I guess we have six cabinets there>

In Example 5-5 and Example 5-6 respectively, Sarah and Tanaka use the American back-channel strategy of following topic openings with back-channels. As discussed previously, it is critical for American leaders to know whether or not supporters are familiar with the topic that is initiated. As the officers-in-charge, Ito and Claire, check for topic recognition by following their topic openings with short pauses, and the supporters, Sarah and Tanaka, respond with back-channels. The officers-in-charge then continue with the details of their topics. Thus, both the American and Japanese officers sometimes display their support in similar ways as they encourage the talk of an officer-in-charge by following openings with back-channels. Such a similarity most likely occurs because the round structure is observed in both cross-cultural meetings; as the American and Japanese officers open their own topics according to a predefined agenda, they are prompted to follow the structural organization prescribed by an American system.

The Japanese Strategy

Following topic openings, the Japanese officers continue to back-channel in the context of topical points. For example, Example 5-7 shows that Tanaka back-channels four times in the context of Cindy's topic about expense reimbursements in the Corporate Banking Meeting.

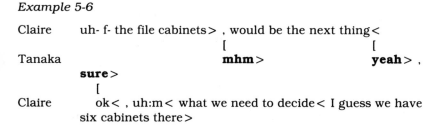

Example 5-7

Cindy	and then I talked to Susie Studbhol< , in
	[
Tanaka	**mhm**>
Cindy	Controller's< to- also< get that rolling< as far as
	[
Tanaka	**mhm**<
Cindy	the expense reimbursements< since I've started
	[
Tanaka	**mhm**<
Cindy	getting< some- forms back from the account officers
	[
Tanaka	**mhm**

Following Cindy's opening, "and then I talked to Susie Studbhol," Tanaka tracks each of her points with a "mhm." As Tanaka back-channels, he emphasizes his role as a supporter and therefore, satisfies his native expectation of nonconfrontational interaction. In turn, as Tanaka encourages Cindy to proceed with her delivery of topical points, Cindy is able to accomplish an individual presentation of her own topic. In this cross-cultural encounter, then, it seems that there is a happy medium; both interactants extend their strategies to the interaction, and achieve their native expectations for interaction. Thus, the use of native strategies in cross-cultural interaction does not always result in detrimental consequences.

There are several factors contributing to the general success of the communication in the cross-cultural meetings. First, the conversationalists in both meetings are in nonadversarial roles; both the Americans and the Japanese are members of the same financial institution. As is also the case with the intracultural meetings, these nonoppositional relationships are likely to produce less conflict in personal and institutional expectations than in adversarial setups, such as in "negotiations" where cross-cultural members have distinctly competing interests.

Another influential factor in the cross-cultural meetings may be the linguistic medium of interaction, English, and several structural similarities between these meetings and the intracultural American meeting. Both cross-cultural meetings institute rounds and agendas, and the general organization of the Corporate Banking Meeting in particular closely resembles the intracultural American meeting. For example, unlike the Japanese and Personnel meetings, the Corporate Banking Meeting does not contain an initial nontask sounding topic. The overall similarity in structure of the cross-cultural meetings to the American meeting may be just enough for the Americans to overlook what might otherwise be seen as "excessive" back-channeling by the Japanese. Conversely, for the Japanese, the absence of frequent back-channeling on the part of the American participants may be justifiable in light of the fact that the cross-cultural interaction is in English.

Finally, it may be the degree of unobtrusiveness of the Japanese back-channel strategy itself; unlike their other strategies, frequent back-channeling does not prevent American cross-cultural conversationalists from reaching their goal of delivering their topics independently according to a predefined meeting agenda. Furthermore, back-channels similarly express support for both the Americans and the Japanese, and although each places their back-channels in different contexts, they both contextualize back-channels in short pauses in conversation.

As I look back at cross-cultural conversations between my Japanese family and American friends, I recall several conversations in which my grandmother had skillfully convinced our friends of her ability to speak English. In reality, my grandmother did not *speak* a word of English; she did not *know* English. She had our friends fooled, though, as she carefully placed little vocalizations in the conversational spaces, along with smiles and gentle nods. Later, our friends would tell us, "Grandmother is sweet, but she certainly is quiet!"

CONCLUSION

In conclusion, I discussed the following findings of back-channel comparisons in the intracultural meetings. First, in general, the Japanese supporters back-channeled more than their American counterparts. Second, there was an inverse relationship between back-chaneling and volubility in the Japanese meeting, but not in the American. Finally, the American and Japanese supporters used back-channels in different contexts: the Americans, between topic openings and initial points, but the Japanese, in the context of topical points. I argued that both back-channel strategies support a leading participant's talk, but that such support is expressed to meet different interactional expectations: within-group independence for the Americans; nonconfrontation for the Japanese.

In the cross-cultural meetings, I found that although Americans generally used their own strategies, Japanese combined American and Japanese strategies. The effect of combined strategies was an increase in back-channel frequency by Japanese. As found in White's (1989) study, the accentuated frequency of Japanese supporter back-channels in the cross-cultural meeting did not result in gross misunderstandings. However, the communication between Americans and Japanese in both this study and White's occurred between participants in nonadversarial relationships. In the present study, the meeting participants were co-employees on the same team.

In adversarial business negotiations however, in which Americans and Japanese represent different institutions with competing or conflicting goals, differences in the way support is expressed may present problems for negotiators. In these situations, conversational strategies such as back-channeling that manifest themselves covertly, or below the level of consciousness, may provoke old stereotypes: "Japanese are inscrutable"; "Americans are selfish."

CHAPTER 6

FUTURE STUDIES IN CROSS-CULTURAL COMMUNICATION AND CONVERSATIONAL STRATEGIES

In the foregoing analysis, I compared several strategies that a particular group of Americans and Japanese used to manage topics. I illustrated examples of recurrent strategies found in the data of two intracultural meetings. Again, I want to emphasize that these topic-management strategies, though empirically determined, do not constitute an exhaustive set of strategies. Clearly, there are other strategies that Americans and Japanese frequently and typically use in intracultural business interaction. Such strategies urgently await discovery through further investigation.

Furthermore, grounded in the theoretical framework of interactional sociolinguistics (Gumperz, 1982a; Tannen 1984a), and guided by the Cross-Talk Model (Gumperz, Jupp, and Roberts, 1979), I argued that the American and Japanese topic-management strategies reflect a more profound difference in interactional expectation: within-group independence for Americans, nonconfrontation for Japanese. Informed by the research of other anthropologists, sociologists, and linguists, I conceived these expectations from the interactive dimensions of individuality and collectivity, and talk and silence. Future studies may explore other prominent features of American and Japanese behavior, and the way conversational strategies reflect such sociocultural orientations.

An equally important area of investigation is American-Japanese cross-cultural interaction. Although I suggested several implications through descriptions of observed cross-cultural interaction and findings from the back-up data, more empirical support is needed. With respect to the study of meetings in particular, when cross-cultural data of business meetings at the managerial level conducted in Japanese become available, this may be a potential area of inquiry. Another may be the study of conversational strategies in business interaction in "negotiation" settings or other *soto* (out-group) and adversarial situations where cross-cultural members belong to groups with opposing interests.

The following is a series of more specific questions that warrant attention.

1. What are the differences in native versus nonnative conversational strategies. For Americans? For Japanese?
2. What kind of conversational strategies do non-native speakers of English use? Do they "style-switch" as they might "code-switch"?
   A. If they do, then is such style-switching concurrent with the language being used? What and who does it depend on? When and where does it occur? Why do interactants style switch—does it satisfy an interactional need?
   B. f they don't, is one style systematically used?
   C. If there are those who style-switch and those who "style-extend," what are the differences between these two groups?
3. How do Americans and Japanese respond to each other's conversational strategies in cross-cultural communication? When the medium of interaction is English? Japanese?
4. Does an awareness of differences in conversational strategies benefit cross-cultural interactants?
   A. Can nonnative strategies be learned? Acquired? Are some more easily acquired/learned than others? If so, why?
   B. Can we teach nonnative strategies? If so, which ones? How?

Having asked these questions, here, I probe further into these areas of inquiry. In applied linguistics, it is common to refer to the use of a native-language feature in the target language as "transfer." Brown (1987) and Odlin (1989) among others have described "transfer" as either having a "positive" effect, in which case the native-language code can help in the learning of the target language, or a "negative" one, in which case the native language "interferes" with the learning of the second language. Although this area of inquiry is often restricted to the investigation of the transfer of a linguistic code, a potential area of sociolinguistic investigation that follows from such research in second language learning is, then: Do second language learners "extend" their native conversational strategies in interactions with target language speakers as they might "transfer" a linguistic code?[1] Are "extensions" consistent, or do nonnative speakers "style-switch" as they might "code-switch"? (For studies of code-switching, see for example, Blom and Gumperz, 1986, Gumperz, 1982a, and Nishimura, 1986.) How are "extended" styles evaluated?

The principle of transfer was established in part on Lado's (1957) theory of contrastive analysis. An assumption of contrastive analysis is that the greater the difference between two codes, the more difficult it is for users of one code to learn the other. Although contrastive analysis has fallen from favor in its strong form which claims the ability to predict difficulties, the notion of difference-difficulty is still debated today. What kind of a role does the degree of difference between two cultures, or the degree of "cultural gap" play in learning a nonnative style?

As English is used increasingly as an "international" language (Smith, 1983), the language called "English" has become increasingly pluralistic (Kachru, 1982). Studies of different varieties of English (for example, for Indian English, see Gumperz, Aulakh and Kaltman, 1982; Mishra, 1982) report that cross-cultural miscommunication occur as "nonnative" English speakers systematically use nonmainstream strategies in interaction with "native" speakers of English, and native speakers mistinterpret them. Do extended strategies always result in miscommunication?

A related phenomenon researched in the study of linguistic variation is "hypercorrection" (Labov, 1972); a compensatorial

[1] I have used the term "extension" to describe the use of a native strategy in cross-cultural interaction to differentiate it from the "transfer" of a linguistic code. Moreover, my feeling on "extensions" is that they do not always result in "interference" in cross-cultural communication as does "negative transfer" communication in a target language.

behavior in which nonnative speakers of English or speakers of a nonstandard variety of English attempt to correct their linguistic forms (phonological, lexical, and grammatical) to conform to a prestige variety. The result is an exaggerated, hypercorrected manifestation of the standard variety. In learning a second language, do nonnative speakers hypercorrect communicative styles? My hypothetical question is engendered by several casual observations of Japanese in interaction with Americans. I have noticed on occasion the highly antagonistic and aggressive behavior of Japanese in English interaction. The same Japanese would then be agreeable in interaction in Japanese. What factors are at play which create such a difference in interactional style?

Finally, in terms of pedagogy: Can nonnative strategies be taught in a classroom? If so, what kinds of strategies should we include in our programs of second language learning? How can we teach them? These questions occurred to me when I was teaching Japanese in an American high school. One day, as pairs finished performing their assigned dialogs in front of the class, the students asked in their typical curious fashion, "So what did we get? Who did the best?" As instructed by the administration, I made sure to "encourage" them by telling them they all did well, and then pointed out two pairs that I thought were particularly exceptional. An eager student from one of these two groups then leaped up and challenged his competitors, "We should have a *speak-off!*" As I took a moment to figure out exactly what a "speak-off" is, I was amused and impressed that the young student had so profoundly incorporated in his style of communication the importance of the "eloquent speaker." On the other hand, I was somewhat disturbed as I came to the realization that "eloquent speakership" was in fact what I had been teaching them. As I have argued, in contrast to the American esteem of the "eloquent speaker," Japanese place a more significant emphasis on listenership. For second language learners of Japanese, then, a major aim might be to become "a good listener" (Szatrowski, 1989:33). Thus, a pedagogical challenge is how Japanese language teachers might teach a "listening style"; one which goes above and beyond the "listening comprehension" exercises that we so often include as a basic part of our "four skill" language programs.

These are a small sample of questions that might be addressed in future research on American and Japanese conversational strategies. In addition to these, conversational strategies may be explored in other genres, channels, and settings, with different kinds of participants and through varied methodological approaches. Moreover, although the body of research in sociolinguistics and linguistic anthropology continues to grow, there is still a need for interpretive investigation of different languages and the way in which they are contextualized in a variety of societies and cultures.

This study is a modest example of how a particular group of American and Japanese bank officers tried to resolve their double binds through culture-specific topic-management strategies. The Americans used their strategies to respond to their double bind of the simultaneous need to maintain the integrity of the individual and the rapport of the group through the same medium: talk. The Japanese used their strategies in reacting to the dilemma of having to emphasize the group through a medium that is viewed negatively: talk. Thus, the balance of the individual and the group, and talk and silence, pose a problem for both Americans and Japanese alike: "Damned if you do; damned if you don't." As members of these groups, each constructs a portrait of the dissonant self. Our cultural lives are different, perhaps extremely different, but on the note of internal discord we are all the same. Unraveling the tangles of difference from sameness, of lines from circles, is the investigative expanse of interactional sociolinguistics, conversation analysis, and cross-cultural communication.

REFERENCES

Althen, G. (1988). *American ways: A guide for foreigners in the United States.* Yarmouth, ME: Intercultural Press.

Arima, M. (1989). Japanese culture versus schizophrenic interpretation. *Text, 9*(3), 351-65.

Atkinson, J. M., & Heritage, J. (1984). *Structure of social action: Studies in conversation analysis.* Cambridge: Cambridge University Press.

Atkinson, M. A., Cuff, E. C., & Lee, J. R. E. (1978). The recommencement of a meeting as a member's accomplishment. In J. Schenkein (Ed.), *Studies in the organization of conversational interaction* (pp. 133-153). New York: Academic Press.

Barnlund, D. C. (1975). Verbal self-disclosure: Topics, targets, depth. In L. F. Luce & E. C. Smith (Eds.), *Toward internationalism: Readings in cross-cultural communication* (2nd ed., pp. 147-165).

Bateson, G. (1972). *Steps to an ecology of mind.* New York: Ballantine.

______. (1979). *Mind and nature: A necessary unity.* New York: Dutton.

Becker, A. L. (1988). Language in particular: A lecture. In D. Tannen (Ed.), *Linguistics in context: Connecting observation and understanding* (pp. 17-36). Norwood, NJ: Ablex.

Befu, H. (1986). An ethnography of dinner entertainment in Japan. In T. S. Lebra & W. P. Lebra (Eds.), *Japanese culture and behavior: Selected readings* (pp. 108-120). Honolulu, HI: University of Hawaii Press.

Bennett, A. (1981). Interruptions and the interpretation of conversation. *Discourse Processes, 4*, 171-88.

Bennett, J. W., & Ishino, I. (1963). *Paternalism in the Japanese economy.* Minneapolis: University of Minnesota Press.

Blom, J., & Gumperz, J. J. (1986). Social meaning in linguistic structures: Code-switching in Norway. In J. J. Gumperz & D. Hymes (Eds.), *Directions in sociolinguistics* (pp. 407-34). Oxford: Basil Blackwell.

Bowers, J. R. (1988). Japan-U.S. relationships from an intercultural communication point of view. *The Language Teacher, 12*(5), 17-22.

Brown, G., & Yule, G. (1983). *Discourse analysis*. Cambridge: Cambridge University Press.

Brown, H. D. (1987). *Principles of language learning and teaching*. Englewood Cliffs, NJ: Prentice-Hall.

Brown, P., & Levinson, S. C. (1987). *Politeness: Some universals in language usage*. Cambridge: Cambridge University Press.

Button, G., & Casey, N. (1984). Generating the topic: The use of topic initial elicitors. In M. J. Atkinson & J. Heritage (Eds.), *Structure of social action: studies in conversation analysis* (pp. 167-90). Cambridge: Cambridge University Press.

______. (1988/89). Topic initiation: Business-at-hand. *Research on Language and Social Interaction, 22*, 61-92.

______, & Lee, J. R. E. (Eds.). (1987). *Talk and social organisation*. Philadelphia: Multilingual Matters.

Carbaugh, D. (1988). *Talking American: Cultural discourses on Donahue*. Norwood, NJ: Ablex.

Cathcart, D., & Cathcart, R. (1982). Japanese social experience and concept of groups. In L. A. Samovar & R. E. Porter (Eds.), *Intercultural communication: A reader* (pp. 120-29). Belmont, CA: Wadsworth.

Chafe, W. (1976). Givenness, constrastiveness, definiteness, subjects, topics and point of view. In C. N. Li (Ed.), *Subject and topic* (pp. 27-55). New York, NY: Academic Press.

______. (1979). The flow of thought and the flow of language. In T. Givon (Ed.), *Syntax and Semantics, 12* (pp. 159-81). New York: Academic Press.

______. (Ed.). (1980). *The pear stories*. Norwood, NJ: Ablex.

______. (1985). Linguistic differences produced by differences between speaking and writing. In D. R. Olson, N. Torrance, & A. Hildyard (Eds.), *Literacy, language, and learning: The nature of consequences of reading and writing* (pp. 105-23). Cambridge: Cambridge University Press.

Chambers, G. S., & Cummings, W. K. (1990). *Profiting from education: Japan-United States international educational ventures in the 1980s*. New York: Institute of International Education.

Clancy, P. (1972). Analysis of a conversation. *Anthropological Linguistics, 14*, 78-86.

______. (1980). Referential choice in English and Japanese narrative discourse. In W. Chafe (Ed.), *The pear stories* (pp. 127-202). Norwood, NJ: Ablex.

______. (1982). Written and spoken style in Japanese narratives. In D. Tannen (Ed.), *Spoken and written language* (pp. 55-76). Norwood, NJ: Ablex.

Condon, J. C., & Saito, M. (Eds.). (1974). *Intercultural encounters with Japan*. Tokyo: The Simul Press.

Crystal, D. (1986). *A dictionary of linguistics and phonetics* (2nd ed.). Oxford: Basil Blackwell.

Cuff, C., & Sharrock, W. W. (1985). Meetings. In T. A. Van Dijk (Ed.), *Handbook of discourse analysis: Discourse and dialogue* (Vol. 3, pp. 149-59). London: Academic Press.

Danes, F. (1974). Functional sentence perspective and the organization of the text. In F. Danes (Ed.), *Papers on functional sentence perspective* (pp. 106-28). Prague: Academic Publishing House of the Czechoslovak Academy of Sciences.

De Mente, B. L. (1989). *Businessman's guide to Japan: Opening doors . . . and closing deals!* Vermont and Tokyo: Yenbooks.
Denny, R. (1985). Marking the interaction order: The social constitution of turn exchange and speaking turns. *Language in Society, 14*, 41-62.
Doi, T. (1971). *Amae on Koozoo* (The structure of 'amae'). Tokyo: Koobundoo.
______. (1973). *The anatomy of dependence* (J. Bester, trans.). Tokyo: Kodansha.
______. (1974). Some psychological themes in Japanese human relationships. In J. C. Condon & M. Saito (Eds.), *Intercultural encounters with Japan* (pp. 17-26). Tokyo: The Simul Press.
______. (1982). The Japanese patterns of communicating the the concept of amae. In L. A. Samovar & R. E. Porter (Eds.), *Intercultural communication: A reader* (pp. 218-222). Belmont, CA: Wadsworth.
______. (1986). Amae: A key concept for understanding Japanese personality structure. In T. S. Lebra & W. P. Lebra (Eds.), *Japanese culture and behavior: Selected readings* (pp. 121-129). Honolulu: University of Hawaii Press.
Duncan, S., Jr. (1973). Toward a grammar for dyadic conversation. *Semiotica, 9*(1), 29-46.
______, & Fiske, D. W. (1977). *Face-to-face interaction: Research, methods, and theory*. Hillsdale, NJ: Lawrence Erlbaum.
______. (1985). *Interaction structure and strategy*. Cambridge: Cambridge University Press.
Edelsky, C. (1981). Who's got the floor? *Language in Society, 10*, 383-421.
Edmonson, W. (1981). *Spoken discourse: A model for analysis*. London and New York: Longman.
Elzinga, R. H. (1978). Temporal organization of conversation. *Sociolinguistics Newsletter, 9*(2), 29-31.
Erickson, F. (1976). Gatekeeping encounters: A social selection process. In P. R. Sanday (Ed.), *Anthropology and the public interest* (pp. 111-145). New York: Academic Press.
______. (1979). Talking down: Some cultural sources of miscommunication in interracial interviews. In A. Wolfgang (Ed.), *Nonverbal behavior: Applications and cultural implications* (pp. 99-126). New York: Academic Press.
______. (1982). Money tree, lasagna bush, salt and pepper: Social construction of topical cohesion in a conversation among Italian-Americans. In D. Tannen (Ed.), *Analyzing discourse: Text and talk* (Georgetown University Round Table on Languages and Linguistics) (pp. 43-70). Washington, DC: Georgetown University Press.
______. (1985). Listening and speaking. Languages and Linguistics: In D. Tannen & J. E. Alatis (Eds.), *The interdependence of theory, data and application* (Georgetown University Round Table on Languages and Linguistics 1985) (pp. 294-319). Washington, DC: Georgetown University Press.
______, & Schultz, J. (1982). *The counselor as gatekeeper: Social interaction in interviews*. New York: Academic Press.
Fallows, J. (1989). *More like us: Making America great again*. Boston: Houghton Mifflin.
Fiksdal, S. R. (1986). *The right time and pace: A microanalysis of cross-cultural gatekeeping interviews* (Doctoral dissertation, University of Michigan, 1981). *Dissertation Abstracts International, 47*, 07A.
Fisiak, J. (Ed.). (1980). *Theoretical issues in contrastive linguistics*. Amsterdam: John Benjamins.

Foster, S. (1982). Learning to develop a topic. *Papers and Reports on Child Language Development, 21*, 73-70.
Friday, R. A. (1989). Contrasts in discussion behaviors of German and American managers. *International Journal of Intercultural Relations, 13*, 429-46.
Fruin, M. W. (1983). *Kikkoman: Company, clan and community*. Cambridge, MA: Harvard University Press.
Gallois, C., & Markel, N. N. (1975). Turn taking: Social personality and conversational style. *Journal of Personality and Social Psychology, 31*, 1134-40.
Garfinkel, H. (1967). *Studies in ethnomethodology*. Englewood Cliffs, NJ: Prentice-Hall.
_____. (1986). Remarks on ethnomethodology. In J. J. Gumperz & D. Hymes (Eds.), *Directions in sociolinguistics* (pp. 301-21). Oxford: Basil Blackwell.
Geertz, C. (1973). *The interpretation of cultures*. New York: Basic Books.
_____. (1983). *Local knowledge: Further essays in interpretive anthropology*. New York: Basic Books.
_____. (1984). "From the native's point of view": On the nature of anthropological understanding. In R. A. Shweder & R. A. LeVine (Eds.), *Culture theory: Essays on mind, self, and emotion* (pp. 123-36). Cambridge: Cambridge University Press.
Giglioli, P. P. (1972). *Language and social context*. Harmondsworth, Middlesex: Penguin Books.
Givon, T. (1983). Topic continuity in discourse: An introduction. In T. Givon (Ed.), *Topic continuity in discourse: A quantitative cross-language study* (pp. 11-42). Amsterdam/Philadelphia: John Benjamins.
Goffman, E. (1955). On face-work: Analysis of ritual elements in social interaction. *Psychiatry, 18*, 213-31.
_____. (1959). *The presentation of self in every day life*. New York: Doubleday.
_____. (1963). *Behavior in public places: Notes on the social organization of gatherings*. Glencoe, IL: The Free Press of Glencoe.
_____. (1967). *Interaction ritual*. New York: Doubleday.
_____. (1972). The neglected situation. In P. P. Giglioli (Ed.), *Language and social context* (pp. 61-6). Harmondsworth, Middlesex: Penguin Books.
_____. (1974). *Frame analysis*. New York: Harper and Row.
_____. (1981). *Forms of talk*. Philadelphia: University of Pennsylvania Press.
Goodwin, M. H. (1980). Processes of mutual monitoring implicated in the production of description sequences. *Sociological Inquiry, 50*, 303-17.
Grice, P. H. (1975). Further notes on logic and conversation. In P. Cole & J. Morgan (Eds.), *Syntax and semantics* (Vol. 9: Pragmatics, pp. 113-27). New York: Academic Press.
Grimes, J. (1982). Topics within topics. In D. Tannen (Ed.), *Analyzing discourse: Text and talk* (Georgetown University Round Table on Languages and Linguistics) (pp. 164-76). Washington, DC: Georgetown University Press.
Gumperz, J. J. (1972). The speech community. In P. P. Giglioli (Ed.), *Language and social context* (pp. 219-31). Harmondsworth, Middlesex: Penguin Books.
_____. (1976). Language, communication, and public negotiation. In P. R. Sanday (Ed.), *Anthropology and the public interest* (pp. 273-94). New York: Academic Press.
_____. (1978). Conversational analysis of interethnic communication. In E. L. Ross (Ed.), *Interethnic dommunication* (pp. 13-31). (Southern Anthropolog-

ical Society Proceedings, No. 12). Athens, GA: University of Georgia Press.
______. (1982a). *Discourse strategies*. Cambridge: Cambridge University Press.
______. (1982b). Fact and inference in courtroom testimony. In J. J. Gumperz (Ed.), *Language and social identity* (pp. 163-95). Cambridge: Cambridge University Press.
______. (Ed.). (1982c). *Language and social identity*. Cambridge: Cambridge University Press.
______, & Cook-Gumperz, J. (1982a). Introduction: Language and the communication of social identity. In J. J. Gumperz (Ed.), *Language and social identity* (pp. 1-21). Cambridge: Cambridge University Press.
______, & Cook-Gumperz, J. (1982b). Interethnic communication in committee negotiations. In J. J. Gumperz (Ed.), *Language and social identity* (pp. 145-162). Cambridge: Cambridge University Press.
______, Aulakh, G., & Kaltman, H. (1982). Thematic structure and progression in discourse. In J. J. Gumperz (Ed.), *Language and social identity* (pp. 22-56). Cambridge: Cambridge University Press.
______, & Hymes, D. (Eds.). (1986). *Directions in sociolinguistics: The ethnography of communication*. Oxford & New York: Basil Blackwell.
______, Jupp, T. C., & Roberts, C. (1979). *Crosstalk: A study of cross-cultural communication*. Southall: National Centre for Industrial Language Training.
Haarmann, H. (1989). *Symbolic values of foreign language use: From the Japanese case to a general sociolinguistic perspective*. Berlin/New York: Mouton de Gruyter.
Haga, Y. (1985). *Hanase ba Wakaru ka*. Tokyo: Koodansha.
Hall, E. T. (1959). *The silent language*. Garden City, NY: Anchor Press/Doubleday.
______. (1966). *Hidden dimension*. Garden City, NY: Anchor Press/Doubleday.
______. (1977). *Beyond culture*. Garden City, NY: Anchor Press/Doubleday.
______, & Hall, M. R. (1987). *Hidden differences: Doing business with the Japanese*. Garden City, NY: Anchor Press/Doubleday.
Halliday, M. A. K. (1967). Notes on transitivity and them in English: Part 2. *Journal of Linguistics*, *3*, 199-244.
______. (1978). *Language as social semiotic*. London: Edward Arnold.
Harris, P. R., & Morgan, R. T. (Eds.). (1987). Japan, doing business with Asians—Japan/China/Pacific Basin. In P. R. Harris & R. T. Morgan (Eds.), *Managing cultural differences* (pp. 387-98). Houston: Gulf.
Hayashi, R. (1988). Simultaneous talk—from the perspective of floor management of English and Japanese speakers. *World Englishes*, *7*(3), 269-88.
Heritage, J. (1984). *Garfinkel and ethnomethodology*. Cambridge: Polity Press.
Hinds, J. (1977). Paragraph structure and pronominalization. *Papers in Linguistics*, *10*, 77-99.
______. (1978a). Conversational structure: An investigation based on Japanese discourse. In J. Hinds & I. Howard (Eds.), *Problems in Japanese syntax and semantics* (pp. 79-121). Tokyo: Kaitakusha.
______. (1978b). Anaphora in Japanese conversation. In J. Hinds (Ed.), *Anaphora in discourse* (pp. 136-79). Alberta: Linguistic Research.
______. (1980). Japanese conversation, discourse structure and ellipsis. *Discourse Processes*, *3*, 263-86.
______. (1982). *Ellipsis in Japanese*. Carbondale and Edmonton: Linguistic Research.
______. (1983). Topic continuity in Japanese. In T. Givon (Ed.), *Topic continuity*

in discourse (pp. 43-93). Amsterdam: John Benjamins.

______. (1986). *Japanese*. London: Croom Helm.

______, & Hinds, W. (1979). Participant identification in Japanese narrative discourse. In G. Bedell, E. Kobayashi, & M. Muraki (Eds.), *Explorations in linguistics: Papers in honor of Kazuko Inoue* (pp. 201-12). Tokyo: Kenkyuusha.

Hosokawa, H. (1990). Japanese demonstratives ko-, so-, and a-. *The Georgeown Journal of Languages and Linguistics, 1*(2), 169-78.

Hymes, D. (1962). The ethnography of speaking. In T. Gladwin & W. C. Sturtevant (Eds.), *Anthropology and human behavior* (pp. 13-53). Washington, DC: Anthropological Society of Washington.

______. (1964). Toward ethnographies of communication: The analysis of communicative events. In P. P. Giglioli (Ed.), *Language and social context* (pp. 21-44). Harmondsworth: Penguin Books.

______. (1986). Models of the interaction of language and social life. In J. J. Gumperz & D. Dell Hymes (Eds.), *Directions in sociolinguistics: The ethnography of communication* (pp. 35-71). New York: Basil Blackwell.

Ikegami, Y. (1989). Introduction. Discourse analysis in Japan. Special Issue, *Text, 9*(3), 263-73.

Ishida, T. (1984). Conflict and its accommodation: Omote-ura and uchi-soto relations. In E. S. Krauss, T. P. Rohlen, & P. G. Steinhoff (Eds.), *Conflict in Japan* (pp. 16-38). Honolulu, HI: The University of Hawaii Press.

Ishii, S. (1984). Enryo-sasshi communication: A key to understanding Japanese interpersonal relations. *Cross Currents, 1*(11), 49-58.

Jameson, S., & Schoenberger, K. (1988, August 11). Japanese find U.S. workers a puzzling lot. *Washington Post*.

Kachru, B. B. (1982). *The other tongue: English across cultures*. Oxford and New York: Pergamon Press.

Kato, H. (1957). Aru kazoku no komyunikeishon seikatsu (Communication behavior in family life). *Shisoo*, pp. 92-108.

Keenan, E. O., & Schieffelin, B. B. (1975). Topic as a discourse notion: A study of topic in the conversations of children and adults. In C. N. Li (Ed.), *Subject and topic* (pp. 335-84). New York: Academic Press.

Kindaichi, H. (1957). *Nihongo*. Tokyo: Iwanami.

Kondo, D. K. (1990). *Crafting selves: Power, gender and discourses of identity in a Japanese workplace*. Chicago, IL: University of Chicago Press.

Kume, T. (1985). Managerial attitudes toward decision-making: North America and Japan. In W. B. Gudykunst, L. P. Stewart, & S. Ting-Toomey (Eds.), *Communication, culture and organizational processes* (pp. 231-251). Beverly Hills/London: Sage.

Kumon, S. (1982). Some Principles Governing the Thought and Behavior of Japanese (contextualists). *The Journal of Japanese Studies, 8*(1), 5-28.

Kuno, S. (1973). *The structure of the Japanese language*. Cambridge, MA: The MIT Press.

______. (1987). *Functional syntax: Anaphora, discourse and empathy*. Chicago: The University of Chicago Press.

______, & Kaburaki, E. (1977). Empathy and syntax. *Linguistic Inquiry, 8*(4), 627-72.

Labov, W. (1972). *Sociolinguistic patterns*. Philadelphia, PA: University of Philadelphia Press.

Lado, R. (1957). *Linguistics across cultures*. Ann Arbor, MI: The University of Michigan Press.

Lakoff, R. (1972). Language in context. *Language, 48*(4), 907- 27.

______. (1979). Stylistic strategies within a grammar of style. In J. Orasanu, M. Slater, & L. L. Adler (Eds.), *Language, Sex and Gender. Annals of the New York Academy of Science, 327*, 53-78.

Lebra, T. S. (1984). Nonconfrontational strategies for management of interpersonal conflicts. In E. S. Krauss, T. P. Rohlen, & P. G. Steinhoff (Eds.), *Conflict in Japan* (pp. 41-60). Honolulu, HI: The University of Hawaii Press.

______. (1986). *Japanese patterns of behavior* (5th ed.). Honolulu, HI: University of Hawaii Press.

______. (1987). The cultural significance of silence in Japanese communication. *Multilingua, 6*(4), 343-57.

______, & Lebra, W. P. (Eds.). (1986). *Japanese culture and behavior: Selected readings*. Honolulu, HI: University of Hawaii Press.

Leech, G. N. (1983). *Principles of pragmatics*. London and New York: Longman.

Leff, L. (1989, September 3). Neighbors fight plan to open Japanese school in Maryland. *Washington Post.*

LoCastro, V. (1987). Aizuchi: A Japanese conversational routine. In L. E. Smith (Ed.), *Discourse across cultures* (pp. 101-13). London: Prentice Hall.

Maltz, D. N., & Borker, R. A. (1982). A cultural approach to male-female miscommunication. In J. J. Gumperz (Ed.), *Language and social identity* (pp. 196-216). Cambridge: Cambridge University Press.

March, R. M. (1988). *The Japanese negotiator: Subtlety and strategy beyond Western logic*. Tokyo and New York: Kodansha International.

Martin, J. (1990, April 15). The business of being polite. *The Washington Post.*

Matsumoto, M. (1988). *The unspoken way*. Tokyo and New York: Kodansha.

Matsumoto, Y. (1988). Reexamination of the universality of face: Politeness phenomena in Japanese. *Journal of Pragmatics, 12*, 403-426.

Maynard, D. W. (1980). Placement of topic changes in conversation. *Semiotica, 30*(3/4), 263-90.

Maynard, S. K. (1981). The given/new distinction and the analysis of the Japanese particles -wa and -ga. *Papers in Linguistics: International Journal of Human Communication, 14*(1), 109-30.

______. (1983). *Functions of repetition in Japanese spoken discourse*. Paper read at the Conference on Japanese and Korean Linguistics and Language Teaching at Harvard University, Cambridge, MA.

______. (1985). Review of: Ellipsis in Japanese, by John Hinds. *Journal of Pragmatics, 9*, 847-62.

______. (1986a). Interactional aspects of thematic progression in English casual conversation. *Text, 6*(1), 73-105.

______. (1986b). On back-channel behavior in Japanese and English casual conversation. *Linguistics, 24*, 85-114.

______. (1987). Thematization as a staging device in the Japanese narrative. In J. Hinds, S. K. Maynard, & S. Iwasaki (Eds.), *Perspective on topicalization: The case of Japanese 'wa'* (pp. 57-82). Amsterdam/Philadelphia: John Benjamins.

______. (1988). Pragmatics of interactional signs: A case of uh- huh's and the like in Japanese conversation. *The Fourteenth LACUS Forum*, pp. 67-76. Lake Bluff, IL.

______. (1989). *Japanese conversation: Self-contextualization through structure and interactional management*. Norwood, NJ: Ablex.

McCreary, D. R. (1986). Vygotskyan sociolinguistic theory applied to negotia-

tion in Japanese society. *Language Sciences*, *8*(2), 141-51.
Mehan, H. (1980). *Learning lessons*. Cambridge, MA: Harvard University Press.
Michaels, S., & Collins, J. (1984). Oral discourse styles: Classroom interaction and the acquisition of literacy. In D. Tannen (Ed.), *Coherence in spoken and written discourse* (pp. 219-44). Norwood, NJ: Ablex.
Mill, J. S. (1859). *On liberty*. London: Penguin Books.
Millard, M. (1990, March 11). Tazuko Shibusawa. *The Japan Times, International Weekly Edition*, Tokyo.
Mishra, A. (1982). Discovering connections. In J. J. Gumperz (Ed.), *Language and social identity* (pp. 57-71). Cambridge: Cambridge University Press.
Mizutani, O. (1979). *Nihongo no Seitai* (Japanese: The Spoken Language in Japanese Life). Tokyo: Sotakusha, Inc.
Moeran, B. (1986). Individual, group and seishin: Japan's internal cultural debate. In T. S. Lebra & W. P. Lebra (Eds.), *Japanese culture and behavior: Selected readings* (pp. 62-79). Honolulu, HI: University of Hawaii Press.
Nakane, C. (1967). *Tateshakai no Ningen-kankei* (Human Relations in a Vertical Society). Tokyo: Koodansha.
_____. (1970). *Japanese society*. Berkeley, CA: University of California Press.
_____. (1972). *Tekioo no Jooken* (Conditions of Adjustment). Tokyo: Koodansha.
_____. (1983). Ie (Household). *Kodansha Encyclopaedia of Japan*, *3*, 259-61.
_____. (1986). Criteria of group formation. In T. S. Lebra & W. P. Lebra (Eds.), *Japanese culture and behavior: Selected readings* (pp. 171-187). Honolulu, HI: University of Hawaii Press.
Namiki, N., & Sethi, S. P. (1988). Japan. In R. Nath (Ed.), *Comparative management: A regional view* (pp. 55-96). Cambridge, MA: Ballinger.
Newsweek. (1990, April 2). What Japan thinks of us: A nation of crybabies? Special Report (pp. 18-25).
Nishimura, M. (1986). Intrasentential code-switching: The case of language assignment. In J. Vaid (Ed.), *Language processing in bilinguals: Psycholinguistic and neuropsychological perspectives* (pp. 123-44). Hillsdale, NJ: Lawrence Erlbaum.
Norrick, N. (1987). Functions of repetition in conversation. *Text*, *7*(3), 245-64.
Odlin, T. (1989). *Language transfer*. Cambridge: Cambridge University Press.
Okabe, R. (1983). Cultural assumptions of east and west: Japan and the United States. In W. B. Gudykunst (Ed.), *Intercultural communication theory* (pp. 21-44). Beverly Hills/London/New Delhi: Sage.
Okazaki, S. (1990). *Participants' roles and floor management in Japanese-English bilingual conversation*. Unpublished manuscript. Georgetown University, Washington, DC.
Ouchi, W. G. (1981). *Theory Z*. Reading, MA: Addison-Wesley.
Pfeiffer, J. (1988, January). How not to lose the trade wars by cultural gaffes. *Smithsonian*, pp. 145-56.
Philips, S. U. (1972). Participant structures and communicative competence: Warm Springs children in community and classroom. In C. Cazden, V. John, & D. Hymes (Eds.), *Functions of language in classroom* (pp. 370-94). New York: Teachers College Press.
_____. (1976). Some sources of cultural variability in the regulation of talk. *Language in Society*, *5*, 81-95.
_____. (1983). *The invisible culture: Communication in classroom and community on the Warm Springs Indian Reservation*. New York: Longman.
_____. (1985). Interaction structured through talk and interaction structured

through "silence." In D. Tannen & M. Saville-Troike (Eds.), *Perspectives on silence* (pp. 205-214). Norwood, NJ: Ablex.

_____. (1989). Warm Springs 'Indian Time': How the regulation of participation affects the progress of events. In R. Bauman & J. Sherzer (Eds.), *Explorations in the ethnography of speaking* (pp. 92-109). Cambridge: Cambridge University Press.

Polanyi, L. (1985). Conversational storytelling. In T. A. van Dijk (Ed.), *Handbook of discourse analysis: Discourse and dialogue* (pp. 183-202). London: Academic Press.

_____. (1989). *Telling the American story: A structural and cultural analysis of conversational storytelling.* Cambridge, MA: The MIT Press.

Przeworski, A., & Teune, H. (1970). *The logic of comparative social inquiry: Comparative studies in behavioral science.* New York, NY: Wiley-Interscience.

Ross, E. L. (1978). Interethnic communication: An overview. In E. L. Ross (Ed.), *Interethnic communication* (pp. 1-11). (Southern Anthropological Society Proceedings, No. 12.) Athens, GA: University of Georgia Press.

Sacks, H. (1986). On the analyzability of stories by children. In J. J. Gumperz & D. Hymes (Eds.), *Directions in sociolinguistics: The Ethnography of communication* (pp. 325-45). Oxford & New York, NY: Basil Blackwell.

_____, Schegloff, E., & Jefferson, G. (1974). A simplest systematics for the organization of turn-taking for conversation. *Language*, *50*(4), 696-735.

Saville-Troike, M. (1982). *The ethnography of communication.* Oxford & New York, NY: Basil Blackwell.

_____. (1985). The place of silence in an integrated theory of communication. In D. Tannen (Ed.), *Perspectives on silence* (pp. 3-20). Norwood, NJ: Ablex.

Schank, R. C., & Abelson, R. (1977). *Scripts, plans, goals and understanding.* Hillsdale, NJ: Erlbaum.

Schegloff, E. & Sacks, H. (1982). Opening up closings (Expanded version). In J. Baugh & J. Sherzer (Eds.), *Language in use* (pp. 69-99). New York: Prentice Hall.

Schiffrin, D. (1985). *An empirical basis for discourse pragmatics.* Talk presented at Ferguson-Greenberg Lecture Series, Stanford University, Stanford.

_____. (1987). *Discourse markers. Studies in interactional sociolinguistics.* Cambridge: Cambridge University Press.

Schooler, C. (1989). Review of: The Japanese psyche: Major motifs in the fairy tales of Japan by Hayao Kawai. *The Journal of Asian Studies*, *48*(4), 866-7.

Scollon, R. (1985). The machine stops: Silence in the metaphor of malfunction. In D. Tannen & M. Saville-Troike (Eds.), *Perspectives on silence* (pp. 21-30). Norwood, NJ: Ablex.

_____, & Scollon, S. B. K. (1981). *Narrative, literacy and face in interethnic communication.* Norwood, NJ: Ablex.

Shibamoto, J. S. (1984). Subject ellipses and topic in Japanese. In S. Miyagawa & C. Kitagawa (Eds.), *Studies in Japanese language use* (pp. 233-66). Carbondale, IL, & Edmonton, Canada: Linguistic Research.

Shultz, J. J., Florio, S., & Erickson, F. (1982). Where's the floor? Aspects of the cultural organization of social relationships in communication at home and in school. In P. Gilmore & A. Glatthorn (Eds.), *Ethnography and education: Children in and out of school* (pp. 88-123). Washington, DC: Center for Applied Linguistics (distributed by Ablex, Norwood, NJ).

Shuy, R. W. (1974). *Problems of communication in the cross-cultural medical interview* (Working papers in sociolinguistics, no. 19). Paper presented at the Southwest Educational Development Laboratory. Austin, TX.

______. (1982). Topic as a unit of analysis in a criminal law case. In D. Tannen (Ed.), *Analyzing discourse: Text and talk* (Georgetown University Round Table on Languages and Linguistics) (pp. 113-26). Washington, DC: Georgetown University Press.

______. (1986). *Language crime. Intelligence analysis of tape recorded conversations.* Unpublished manuscript, Georgetown University, Washington, DC.

Shweder, R. A. (1984). Anthropology's romantic rebellion against the enlightenment, or there's more to thinking than reason and evidence. In R. A. Shweder & R. A. LeVine (Eds.), *Culture theory: Essays on mind, self, and emotion* (pp. 27-66). Cambridge: Cambridge University Press.

______, & LeVine, R. A. (1984). *Culture theory: Essays on mind, self, and emotion.* Cambridge: Cambridge University Press.

Smelser, N. J. (1976). *Comparative methods in the social sciences.* Englewood Cliffs, NJ: Prentice-Hall.

Smith, L. E. (1983). *Readings in English as an international language.* Oxford and New York: Pergamon Press.

Smitka, M. (1989). Review of: Information, incentives and bargaining in the Japanese economy by Masahiko Aoki. *The Journal of Asian Studies, 48*(4), 849-50.

Sperber, D., & Wilson, W. (1986). *Relevance: Communication and cognition.* Oxford: Basil Blackwell.

Szatrowski, P. (1989). Aizuchi to sono rizumu (Back-channels and their rhythm). *Gekkan Nihongo, 3*, 32-5.

Tannen, D. (1979). What's in a frame? Surface evidence for underlying expectations. In R. Freedle (Ed.), *New directions in discourse processing* (pp. 137-81). Norwood, NJ: Ablex.

______. (1981a). New York Jewish conversational style. *International Journal of the Sociology of Language, 30*, 133-49.

______. (1981b). The machine-gun question: An example of conversational style. *Journal of Pragmatics, 5*, 5383-97.

______. (1982a). Ethnic style in male/female conversation. In J. Gumperz (Ed.), *Language and social identity* (pp. 217-31). Cambridge: Cambridge University Press.

______. (Ed.). (1982b). *Analyzing discourse: Text and talk.* (Georgetown University Round Table on Languages and Linguistics). Washington, DC: Georgetown University Press.

______. (1983). When is an overlap not an interruption? One component of conversational style. In R. J. Di Pietro, W. Frawley, & A. Wedel (Eds.), *The first Delaware Symposium on language studies* (pp. 119-129). Newark: University of Delaware Press.

______. (1984a). *Conversational style: Analyzing talk among friends.* Norwood, NJ: Ablex.

______. (1984b). Cross-cultural communication. *CATESOL Occasional Papers, 10*, 1-16.

______. (Ed.). (1984c). *Coherence in spoken and written discourse.* Norwood, NJ: Ablex Publishing.

______. (1985a). Cross-cultural communication. In T. van Dijk (Ed.), *Handbook of discourse analysis, discourse analysis in society* (Vol. 4, pp. 203-15). London & Orlando: Academic Press.

______. (1985b). Frames and Schemas in Interaction. *Quaderni di Semantica, 6*(2), 326-35.

______. (1985c). Silence: Anything but. In D. Tannen & M. Saville-Troike (Eds.), *Perspectives on silence* (pp. 93-112). Norwood, NJ: Ablex.

______. (1986). Discourse in cross-cultural communication. *Special issue of Text, 6*, 2.

______. (1989). *Talking voices: Repetition, dialogue, and imagery in conversational discourse.* Cambridge: Cambridge University Press.

______. (1990). *You just don't understand: Women and Men in conversation.* New York: William Morrow.

______, & Saville-Troike, M. (Eds.). (1985). *Perspectives on silence.* Norwood, NJ: Ablex.

______, & Wallat, C. (1987). Interactive frames and knowledge schemas in interaction: Examples from a medical examination/ interview. *Social Psychology Quarterly, 50*(2), 205-216.

Thian, H. (1988). *Setting up and operating a business in Japan: A handbook for the foreign businessman.* Vermont and Tokyo: Charles E. Tuttle.

Thorpe, D. (1983). *"Letting him down lightly." A training appraisal interview* (NCILT Working Paper 37). London: National Centre for Industrial Language Training.

Tsuda, A. (1984). *Sales talk in Japan and the United States: An ethnographic analysis of contrastive speech events.* Washington, DC: Georgetown University Press.

Tsukatani, T., & O'Brien, F. (1986). *Taking your product into the Japanese market: Knowledge for success.* Tokyo: Japanese Research Institute, and Washington, DC: SIETAR International.

Tung, R. L. (1984). How to negotiate with the Japanese. *California Management Review, 26*(4), 62-77.

Vaid, J. (Ed.). (1986). *Language processing in bilinguals: Psycholinguistic and neuropsychological perspectives.* Hillsdale, NJ: Lawrence Erlbaum.

Van Dijk, T. A. (1982). Episodes as units of discourse analysis. In D. Tannen (Ed.), *Analyzing discourse: Text and talk* (Georgetown University Round Table on Languages and Linguistics) (pp. 177-95). Washington, DC: Georgetown University Press.

Van Zandt, H. E. (1970, November-December). How to negotiate in Japan. *Harvard Business Review*, pp. 45-56.

Wagatsuma, H. (1985). *Nihonjin to Amerikajin: Koku ga Oochigai* (Japanese and Americans: Here's the Big Difference). Tokyo: Bungei Shunju.

Weber, M. (1968). Economy and society. In G. Roth & C. Wittich (Eds.), *An outline of interpretive sociology* (Vol. 1, pp. 4-24). New York: Bedminster Press.

White, S. (1989). Back-channels across cultures: A study of Americans and Japanese. *Language in Society, 18*, 59-76.

Whitehead, A. N. (1978). *Process and reality.* New York and London: The Free Press.

Yamada, H. (1990a). Topic and turn distribution in business meetings: American versus Japanese strategies. *Text, 10*(3), 271-95.

______. (1990b). Topic shifts in American and Japanese business conversations. *Georgetown Journal of Languages and Linguistics, 1*(2), 249-56.

Yngve, V. H. (1970). *On getting a word in edgewise.* Papers from the Sixth Regional Meeting of the Chicago Linguistic Society (pp. 567-77). Chicago: Chicago Linguistic Society.

Author Index

Subject Index